Cultural Anthropology:
An Introduction

Cultural Anthropology

An Introduction

IDA MAGLI

TRANSLATED BY JANET SETHRE

McFarland & Company, Inc., Publishers
Jefferson, North Carolina, and London

An earlier version of this book was first published as
Introduzione all'antropologia culturale:
Storia, aspetti e problemi della teoria della cultura
(Rome and Bari: Laterza, 1980).

Library of Congress Cataloguing-in-Publication Data

Magli, Ida.
    Cultural anthropology : an introduction / Ida Magli ;
translated by Janet Sethre.
      p.   cm.
    Includes bibliographical references and index.
    ISBN 0-7864-0829-4 (softcover : 50# alkaline paper) ∞
    1. Ethnology. 2. Ethnology—History. I. Title.
GN316.M32   2001
306—dc21   00-066453

British Library cataloguing data are available

©2001 Ida Magli. All rights reserved

No part of this book may be reproduced or transmitted in
any form or by any means, electronic or mechanical, including
photocopying or recording, or by any information storage
and retrieval system, without permission in writing from
the publisher.

Manufactured in the United States of America

Cover image ©2001 PhotoSpin

McFarland & Company, Inc., Publishers
  Box 611, Jefferson, North Carolina 28640
  www.mcfarlandpub.com

Table of Contents

Introduction	1
I. The Beginnings of Anthropological Research and the Idea of Progress	
Anthropological Research and Ethnological Research	7
The First Patterns of Human "Progress"	10
A New Intellectual Era	13
II. The Great Journeys: Men Different from Us	
Sixteenth-Century Europe: Breathing the Air of Freedom	17
The First Ethnographic Descriptions and Journey Accounts	21
Around the World with Francesco Gemelli Careri	24
Matteo Ricci's "Adaptation"	26
III. The Seventeenth and Eighteenth Centuries	
Races, Climate, and Relations Among Religions	28
The Great Ocean Voyages and the Work of the "Observateurs de l'Homme"	35
The Dispute Over the "New World"	41
IV. The Nineteenth Century	
The Birth of Linguistic Anthropology	48
Encyclopedic Collections of Klemm and Waitz	59
Evolutionism and Comparativism	63

V. The Classics of Anthropology
Franz Boas   77
  Alfred L. Kroeber   83
  Robert Lowie   92
  Bronislaw Malinowski   97

VI. The Field of Transcendence
The Dispute Over the "Soul" and the Evolution of Religion   111
The Problem of "Potency": Taboo and Mana   116
Hypotheses on Myth   128

VII. Psychology and Anthropology
Psychology and Culture   139
The Problem of Psychiatry and Transcultural Psychiatry   148
Georges Devereux: Normality and Abnormality in Cultures   156

Bibliography   161
Index   169

Introduction

What is cultural anthropology? What relevance can humanity find in having reached—almost before it knew what it was doing—a new level of self-awareness, a new means of objectifying its mode of *being*?

The very adjective "cultural," which we have added to our definition of the human species, appears dramatically generic, inadequate; and today, hardly more than a century after its formulation, even superfluous. Superfluous precisely because human beings are *biologically* cultural. Either anthropology is cultural, or it does not exist.

But have we not always perceived this? Have we not pursued the origins, the most ancient past—any trace of the "human"—on the basis of some environmental transformation? Whether this involved some object defined as "object," which had thus become an instrument, a tool, or else some vague sign considered as "sign," the external projection of a reflected thought, we have always looked to early man's transformation of his environment in searching for his footprints. And once we realized that the past was much more remote than had ever been imagined when following the biblical account, we took as a certain mark of humanity's existence a cranial capacity able to contain a cerebral mass suitable for elaborating "thought." Conscious thought, projecting itself outside the biological organism, and then "re-entering" it (this is the term adopted by the neurobiologist, Gerald Edelman); conscious of its projection: experiencing it, reelaborating it; transforming the environment, objectifying it.

With the birth of cultural anthropology, "culture"—till then considered a kind of "knowledge," and so defined as "civilization," possessed in greater or lesser degree by some human groups and not by others—came to be understood as a distinctive trait of the human species. Therefore all the speculation about human beings which had accumulated for centuries in the area of philosophy suddenly became devoid of any bone structure—that bone structure which philosophers had anxiously sought by asking two fundamental questions to which they never managed to find an answer. The first: What connection is there between what Descartes called *res cogitans* and *res extensa*? The second (Herodotus): Why are people so similar, and yet so different from one another?

The disparity between philosophy and cultural anthropology is incommensurable, precisely because the latter joins the biological organism to its external projection. All aspects of human life are thus included in the definition of "culture." Biology, history, psychology, religion, art, philosophy, and technology continue to subsist as specialized fields of research merely for the convenience of scholars; nonetheless, they are separated from one another only temporarily, their interdependence obliging us to readmit them continually into the Whole. That "complex whole" comprises the first definition of culture, which gave rise to cultural anthropology.

We find here a radical revolution in the philosophy of knowledge: a second revolution, after the one achieved by Aristotle. And in certain ways the new revolutionary path runs in the reverse direction from the one traveled by Aristotle. Aristotle's genius consisted in having realized the need to put in order the indistinct "whole" of nature, by separating its phenomena into different cognitive areas, and defining them with names. With Edward Tylor, anthropology finally found the courage (a thinker becomes a genius only when he possesses courage equal to his intelligence) to reunify all areas of knowledge—even while letting them subsist separately on an analytical level. He accomplished this by demonstrating how, when humanity is involved, the segregation of the disciplines can lead to conclusions that are not so much partial as erroneous. The true problem, in fact, is to understand how areas of knowledge function in their interdependence, since the result is never a product of their sum.

This situation gives rise to the immense richness of anthropological research, ranging from paleontology to archeology, from biology to statistics, from art to religion, from economy to linguistics, from sexuality to politics. All this, though, with a distinctive trait which never abandons it: adherence to a definite object of inquiry, whether a people and its religion, a people and its language, a people and its economy, or a people and its kinship structures. The absolutely pragmatic nature of cultural anthropology—the trait most strongly striking anyone who approaches it—arises from its clinging to concrete behavior, to the daily experience of a given human group, circumscribed in time and space, without drawing general conclusions unless by comparing this behavior and this experience with those of other groups, circumscribed in time and space as well. Comparativism became a scientific method in which, nevertheless, no anthropologist forgot, even for a moment, that what the scholar deduces always remains a mere growth of his capacity for understanding; it does not exist in reality, does not correspond to the behavior of any one group observed as an object of inquiry.

Thus, cultural anthropology is an absolutely new way of studying the human species. It is a way distinguished by a particular history, a particular psycho-cultural attitude: that of Americans. How could we fail to recognize something very American in the obstinate adherence to facts, characterizing cultural anthropologists' research? How could we fail to recognize the Americans' attention to the practical needs of daily living, in the vision of anthropologists who scrupulously note how native peoples "work" in order to obtain food, prepare arrows or fishing hooks, build shelters against the wind and rain? Archeologists, who have now finally stopped asking, with the most improbable suppositions, what the prehistoric religions were, have instead learned from anthropologists to give great attention to "utensils," for we can deduce from them nearly everything about the life of the most ancient peoples: concrete life and, at the same time, "spiritual" life. This, too—the transcendence of the concrete—is a great lesson learned from American anthropology. After a long, fruitless attempt to understand the meaning of the unchanging designs painstakingly woven into blankets by Amerindians, Franz Boas affirmed: "Even designs keep one warm." At that moment, anthropological research revealed its deepest, most explosive power: respect for the other, the recognition of beauty that is intrinsic to the life of humankind, inseparable from the life of any human group.

The desire to "save," to preserve the genuine qualities of what little remains of peoples alienated and defeated in the lands of conquest, has coincided with the objectifying method of science. Thus American anthropologists have found themselves studying their "savages" both from close up and from afar, with advantages and disadvantages, compared to European anthropologists. From close up because, unlike Europeans, scholars like Boas, Alfred L. Kroeber, Ruth Benedict, and Margaret Mead did not usually need to cover great distances to reach their objects of inquiry. From afar because, contrary to the European situation, territorial proximity rendered the "difference" from these fellow inhabitants of the new continent incommensurably more distant and incomprehensible. This explains the American anthropologists' absolute respect for the rules governing research; their observation of the Other, psychologically and intellectually speaking, as if within a science lab, without neglecting the smallest gesture, the most imperceptible of behaviors. What historian had ever noticed that each people possesses an unconscious norm according to which a person stands at a precise, obligatory distance from his interlocutor? Proxemics arose with the American anthropologists. What historian had ever noticed the existence of particular languages assigned to women? Edward Sapir, the most outstanding linguist of the 20th century, not only had an American education, he was also a student of Franz Boas, from whom he learned to consider languages as being constantly linked to the speaker's context. He thus came to perceive the linguistic avoidance of women (*Language and the Woman's Place*, 1975).

Why, then, has America allowed anthropology, its greatest contribution to the reflection and knowledge of man, to fall into almost total neglect? Many factors have certainly acted together in this gradual eclipse; history must still be written on the matter. We can mention here, in our general introduction to the main problems of anthropology, at least one reason worthy of reflection. America is psychologically and culturally so intent on solving practical problems that perhaps it has not fully realized that within the concreteness of anthropological science lies the most important, the most explosive theoretical method of research on humankind, a method which has unhinged all disciplines, forcing them to rethink and reconstruct their patrimony of knowledge. Perhaps this attitude has also been influenced by the silent, slightly impatient assignment to Europeans, by the American academic world, of theoretical thought, as if this were shut up in the truly narrow term of "philosophy."

In turn, Europe has seized on the chance to free itself of an uncomfortable science. Uncomfortable because it emptied folklore—the long-standing, prestigious history of popular traditions—of any meaning. But uncomfortable above all because with the theory of the integrated model of cultural traits, European anthropologists, nearly all of them Marxists, saw the shadow of doubt cast on the very basis of the Marxian explanation of history: a dominant structure, the primacy of the economy.

The introduction to cultural anthropology presented here aims to clarify the formation, history, function, and most relevant results reached in the field of anthropology by referring above all to its origins, and to its most "classic" moment, through its most outstanding and meaningful authors. Particular attention is given to the areas in which anthropology has produced its best fruits. Instead of offering a superficial, all-embracing overview, I have preferred to point out the fundamental problems. I have therefore given a good deal of space to the interpretation of the sacred and of myth, since anthropology deserves credit for having reintroduced the vast relationship with the "plane of potency," present in all societies, in daily life and in the global web of meaning of every culture, by way of ritual, taboo, and myth. A palpable consequence of this new way of studying the entire field of the "sacred," no longer considered as a separate aspect of culture (and therefore not relegated to that particular discipline entitled the "history of religions"), is the rich, fruitful results gained in knowledge of the symbolic meanings of many institutions, and of the intricate interlinking between the concrete, "economic" function and the transcendent, symbolic one.

Emphasis has also been given to the influence that anthropological methods and research have had on psychoanalysis and psychiatry, the interchange among these disciplines proving indispensable.

Finally, I have highlighted the importance of anthropology's relationship to "history"—an importance that has wrought a revolution in all "histories," from art history to political history, from history based on momentous events to the history of long duration. Suffice it to reveal the richness of the anthropological method, which shifted historical research from the classes of the "powerful" to all those about whom history has kept silent for centuries, as if they had never existed: women, children, servants, slaves, and peasants. How can we fail to note how the anthropologist's eye has widened the historian's vision?

This introduction to anthropology has avoided referring to the most recent developments in the discipline, in the wish to highlight, instead, not only what has undoubtedly been accepted in the history of anthropology, but also the problems introduced and left open by the greatest anthropologists—those who seem neglected today. They are deep problems, central to the future of the world, urgent for the future of the West.

It is partly this sense of urgency that leads a European anthropologist to present her work to an American public. With passion.

—Ida Magli, December 2000

CHAPTER I

The Beginnings of Anthropological Research and the Idea of Progress

Anthropological Research and Ethnological Research

Anthropological research is often said to date back to historians such as Herodotus, Strabo, Caesar, and Tacitus, since in their works we find numerous observations on the customs and values of the peoples they describe. However, the analogy is improper, for true anthropological research is marked not by a description of the customs of peoples who are "different" from the observer (such descriptions have never been lacking, because human beings always note their differences from others with surprise, curiosity or fear); but by the emphasis placed on differences or similarities in an effort at self-knowledge, and thus, knowledge of humanity.

In other words, what has distinguished true anthropological research since the era of the great geographical discoveries is not the pure description of habits and customs of different peoples, but the self-doubt which this knowledge arouses in the spirit of thinkers. It is no coincidence that this doubt arises in the same period during which the scientific spirit is being formed (from the end of the 16th century on).

This is also the characteristic distinguishing anthropological research from pure ethnology, since most ethnologists present a simple description of the life of various peoples, without a problematic approach or an attempt at meaningful understanding which leads to comparison. Indeed, we can say that true anthropology was born with the comparative method, and the attempts connected with it to trace a universal history.

These are the reasons why we shall begin our story by defining an awareness of the concept of "culture" as the dividing wall between what is true and proper anthropology, and what is not. In other words, anthropology's existence can be justified in that, at the root of its research, it aims at understanding the global significance of a people's life, calling that significance—though with countless, different shades of meaning—"culture." To retrace the steps of anthropological history therefore implies attempting to determine to what degree individual scholars have been able to grasp the *cultures* of the peoples that they studied, and to what degree, instead, they have limited themselves to describing habits and customs that were found juxtaposed with one another, or else single cultural traits which were not integrated into a unitary model.

Neither shall we begin, then, as is usually done, by indicating in Edward B. Tylor's *Primitive Culture* (1871) the true origin of anthropology—i.e., with the definition of "culture" in its most precise meaning. To do so would be one more symptom of the fact that we are still unable to progress beyond a history ruled by dates, by events, by single famous men; but above all, the concept of culture, though not clearly expressed, was already implicit in the very attitude of the European toward his own history; it was implicit in the increasingly critical awareness of self—an awareness constituting a kind of "cultural destiny." At the end of the 19th century, this awareness had just reached its first stage of growth.

The diversities of appearance and customs distinguishing the peoples of the world were viewed at an early date with intellectual curiosity and philosophical interest on the part of the most active and aggressive nations. Such interest and curiosity were best able to develop where geographic conditions favored wide-ranging observation, and a cognitive attitude in general.

In ancient Egypt a clear idea soon arose concerning the distinguishing traits of several human varieties, while among the ancient Greeks the cognitive attitude influenced men's interest toward human diversities, and even toward certain ethnological theories. The history and literature of the ancient nations of the

Mediterranean area present the richest, most acute observations gathered in the field. As it expanded, Western European civilization confronted an ever greater wealth of information concerning cultural diversities, embracing most of the earth and most of humanity. Whereas the earliest corpus of ethnological knowledge dates back several thousand years, the awareness of its meaning and importance has been apparent for not more than a century; its systematic organization has not yet been totally achieved.

It was an Italian Egyptologist, Ernesto Schiaparelli, who first demonstrated that as early as the first dynasties of the so-called Middle Empire—i.e., from 1400 BC on—the pharaohs organized expeditions to the upper Nile; they were acquainted with the coastal populaces of East Africa, the blacks of Sudan and even the pygmies of the equatorial forests—some of whom, sent off to the pharaoh, aroused great curiosity.

The blacks (Nohesu) are depicted in monumental bas-reliefs in the wall paintings of tombs and in several sculptures. In artistic representations as well as in literary texts, the Egyptians strictly separated the black peoples from the peoples of the North, the Orient and Asia, who, though barbarians and enemies, were still considered to be children of the Sun and of Light, like the Egyptians themselves.

Another famous ethnological document is Chapter 10 of *Genesis*. Here we find no outstanding differences of appearance or customs, but a long list of all the peoples known by the Jews, linking them to Adam by means of their progenitors and founders. The genealogical tradition, according to a custom still extant among herders, served to fix the origins of the tribe and its nobility; to link the races recognized as being most similar, while establishing a distance from the others. At any rate, in the opinion of the Jews, all peoples have an affinity with one another, and the three great primitive branches—those of Shem, Ham and Japheth—equally spread the seed of Adam over the earth. This is the first dogmatic affirmation in history of a rigorous monogenism as regards human origins, and of the fundamental equality of human beings.

We find many traces of the system classifying humanity by progenitors, or eponyms, in Greco-Roman literature as well, in which there are clear echoes of the knowledge acquired from other peoples of the Mediterranean. Thus Homer is acquainted with the

Ethiopians "of burnt face," and the pygmies. Fantastic notions also arose during this period, which would last well into the Middle Ages and beyond. The Ethiopians are described by Herodotus as the largest and finest-looking of all men; it is said of the pygmies that they are forced to fight with cranes, and in the *Odyssey*, we find a whole series of fabulous, monstrous peoples.

Herodotus's descriptive treatises can be compared to the work of a contemporary of his, later said to be Hippocrates of Coo: *De aere, aquis et locis*. It points out the mental and physical differences between Asians and Europeans, and between the inhabitants of single regions as well, attributing such differences to the climate or to nature. This affirmation can be considered as the first one emphasizing the influence of the environment on single peoples.

Hippocrates is often indicated as the precursor of anthropology, but, like other ancient scholars of nature, he ignored the biological concept of race; just as did Aristotle, who in his *Historia animalium*, classified man among the animals, pointing out his principle distinctive traits: relative brain volume, erect posture, capacity to reason, and articulated language.

Differences among men are attributed to the effect of the environment; after Aristotle, the idea of a regular correspondence between latitude and the color of a people is affirmed more and more often. This hypothesis gave rise to the "climate theory," destined to be highly favored for a long time. Simultaneously with reflection on the differences among men, debate proceeded over whether or not man lives in a condition of historical progress. It seems that such a debate has always accompanied humanity's reflections about it. In fact, among the ancients, from Democritus to Plato, from Aristotle to Epicurus, from Cicero to Seneca, we find traces of concepts regarding Progress which are notably similar to those formed in modern times.

The First Patterns of Human "Progress"

Democritus is the first theoretician of that "wild wandering" preceding humanity's achievement of civilized life, under the stimulus of experience and necessity. Plato, in turn, described the cycles of civilization, even going so far as to fix their duration at 9,000 years. Aristotle not only possessed precise concepts—unsurpassed, even today—concerning the power of development and growth which is proper to human thought, but he acutely evaluated the contribution that individuals have brought to the construction of the great collective accomplishments of empirical and pure science.

Epicurus took the further step of eliminating the gods from among the civilizing forces, affirming the exclusive power of Nature and man. Cicero praised new things as being gifted with greater preciseness and safety than ancient ones, and thought it was impossible for the flow of centuries, the help of many geniuses, and such intense study not to lead to any discovery. Seneca, as well, felt sure that men of the future would know more than men of his own time; he even declared that they would marvel at the ignorance of him and his contemporaries concerning things which would be obvious to them.

It is a matter of debate whether the ancients really had an idea of progress (not only as change and increase in the quantity of notions, but also as moral transformation), since in its explicit form, "progress" arises as an idea of the moderns regarding the ancients. The very word *modernus* does not appear until sometime in the fifth or sixth century AD, in texts by the grammarian Priscian and Cassiodorus. It was probably the dissolution of the Roman world and contact with a number of different populations, such as the barbarian, which first led to the idea that the world can change.

But the ancients did not see themselves as "moderns" in contrast with their forefathers, simply because in the reality of collective life there had not been those qualitative changes which applied science would bring to the "modern" world. Until a couple of centuries ago, people's "way of life" was not substantially different from the way it had always been. Things would begin to change only with the first technical applications of steam and electricity.

However, clear traces of the idea of progress marked those philosophies which most strongly perceived the mutation of things and the universality of man. The Stoics, even while remaining fixed in their belief in perennially recurring cycles, possessed some awareness of the existence of the intellectual, moral and social development of humanity. In this, they were followed by the Epicureans.

The most illustrious exponent of the idea of progress in the ancient world is Lucretius, who in the 5th book of his poem on *Nature* formulates the first complete pattern of human progress in collective life. Much more similar to beasts than human beings, the primitives were driven toward civilization—according to Lucretius—by need and experience. Young as the world was young, they knew nothing of agriculture or crafts. They drank from rivers and springs, and ate the raw products of nature, or else hunted wild animals using stones and tree trunks.

They knew nothing of societal life, not yet having discovered its laws. Little by little they learned to build settled homes, abandoning their nomadic origins, and "families" began to form: the first decisive step beyond the life of beasts. The need to indicate objects created language; lightning led people to discover fire, with which they learned to warm themselves, cook food and finally, work metals. Governments arose from the need to put an end to anarchy, but they were founded on the coercion and privilege of the strongest, who soon became the richest as well. After a short time, wealth became an instrument of power; as such it was foolishly desired as a means to conquer happiness.

Just as kingdoms were founded on violence, which was held to be beneficial in the face of the hard necessities of societal life, so religion was born on the basis of fear, and gods arose as a fantastic projection of everything that people wished to be: potent, happy and immortal. Furthermore, the gods represented a path of escape in the solution to the immense mystery of the universe. People imagined that everything depended on the divinities, and placed the gods' abodes in the heavens, raising temples upward, for in the sky they saw the alternation of night and moon, day, sun, rain, snow, wind and lightning. Such a fallacious opinion cast fear into the human heart, and nourished that fear.

Later, people discovered metals: bronze, gold, iron, the ponderous power of silver; and the weapons that rendered wars more uncertain and more ferocious, while life did not become any more joyous. In this respect, progress also marked the corruption of mortals. Though he did not conceive his era as a simple stage on the road to improvement, Lucretius expressed a vision of progress which was not wholly negative. He writes: "Thus, little by little, time draws out of obscurity all things, and knowledge brings them to light; thus men saw things become illuminated, one in the light of the next, till they reached the height of every art."

Lucretius' position, after all, is that of all who weep over the poor use which humanity makes of discoveries, but who cannot help being fascinated by the increase in knowledge and science. Lucretius no longer believes in the classical myth of the golden age, and formulates the hypothesis that human origins were beastly and uncivil. In Lucretius's opinion, the golden age is yet to come, for it will involve moral, not technical, progress; progress linked to Epicurean medicine, that is, to liberation from fear of the gods and death.

For Augustine as well, moral progress and civilization continue to remain distinct. The ingenious vision of Augustine in some ways forms a bridge between Lucretius's premises and the theoreticians of progress in the 18th century. Some foreshadowing of the modern idea of progress can be found as early as Bernard of Chartres (beginning of the 12th century). In his works, progress is depicted as informing the vision of men who are similar to "dwarves standing on the shoulders of giants": men rich with all the experience acquired in the past. On his part, Roger Bacon states: "We are the true ancients"; we can relive the ancients' achievements as if they were wholly our own, and make up for their defects, and take up their toilsome efforts, progressing toward improvement in all fields.

A New Intellectual Era

The debate over the idea of "progress" continued, in its main themes, by way of Descartes, Giordano Bruno, and Blaise Pascal, until the 18th century opened a new intellectual era, with the concept of *evolution*. This concept led to a repudiation of the notion of cyclical time, making way for that of linear time. People began to understand their condition as beings in constant transformation, by following new conceptual pathways: ones which were still confused, still in need of definition.

Anne Robert Turgot tried to design a *Tableau philosophique des progrès successifs de l'esprit humain* (1750), and Marie-Jean-A. Condorcet followed in his steps with his *Tableau historique des progrès de l'esprit humain* (1794), while François-Jean de De Chastellux issued his *Considérations sur le sort des hommes dans les différentes époques de l'histoire* (1772).

At the same time, scholars began to assign classic antiquity an historical place, with respect to other eras. This fact was highly important, because for the first time people freed themselves of schemes which until then had been untouchable, striving to relativize Greco-Roman civilization; in doing so, they paid a price in intellectual audacity which would have been impossible during the preceding century. This effort at comparison can be noted in a number of works. The first in importance and time is Father Lafiteau's *Moeurs des Sauvages Amériquains comparées aux moeurs des premiers temps* (1724). In 1766, with his *L'Antiquité dévoilée,* Nicolas Antoine Boulanger attributes the origin of religious belief to the terrifying memory of the Flood. Boulanger considers that catastrophe as a "revolution in nature," a total shake-up of sky, sea and land; a frightening disease of all creation; and in savages in general, he thinks he recognizes the descendants of the hordes who escaped from the Flood, shaken to such a point as to have fallen into a melancholy languor, incapable of any progress. Antoine Yves Goguet follows with *De l'origine des lois, des arts et des sciences et de leurs progrès chez les anciens peuples* (1778).

Finally, we meet up with the famous analysis by Charles Montesquieu: *Considérations sur les causes de la grandeur et de la décadence des Romains.* These were accounts of the journeys which had led Montesquieu to formulate the climate theory, expressed in a memoir in 1740, *Essai sur les causes qui peuvent affecter les esprits et les caractères,* and taken up later in *L'Esprit des Lois.* His *Lettres Persanes* reflect an analogous influence of exoticism on humanism. In starting from a knowledge of the *Other*, the West now began a critical self-examination.

Other great philosophers reflected on the information now arriving from overseas. Denis Diderot expressed the general themes of an anti-colonialism dictated not by passion, but reason, in his *Supplément au voyage de Bougainville.* Jean-Jacques Rousseau, in turn, made wide usage of travel accounts: he reinterpreted and adopted them to bring some systematic order to the origins of the arts and sciences, and to the origin of human inequality, as well as to reestablish the bases of a social contract.

Voltaire, a "desk ethnologist," reflected on the fact that there are "savages" all over Europe. The peoples of Canada, he wrote, whom we have chosen to call "savages," are infinitely superior to "our" savages. In Voltaire we find a double-edged criticism of European natives: for their technical inferiority, on one hand, and moral inferiority, on the other.

His ideas on cultural evolution are more relevant. In his pamphlet entitled *Lettres chinoises, indiennes et tartares à M. de Pauw par un bénédictin,* he attempts to classify cultural hierarchies, placing the Chinese on the same level with the civilized societies of Europe. His *Essai sur les moeurs* (1756) draws numerous comparisons among peoples, constituting a kind of treatise on comparative civilization. Voltaire has a sense of historical relativity, and understands the meaning of that evolution to which all peoples are beckoned. For centuries, all peoples were what the inhabitants of the southern coasts of Africa and many islands and half of the American population were during Voltaire's time.

Voltaire's position had precedents in the famous "Querelle des anciens et des modernes," which had involved the most eminent thinkers of the 17th century in a dispute going well beyond appearances. It incontestably documented a transformation in world vision, and unmistakably declared its trust in historical "progress"—in man, not as an individual, but as mankind; in the accumulation of knowledge and experience, and so in "science."

Other innovative aspects, in France and abroad, traced the outline of a radically new approach to research. History shook off its historical burden of myth and its dependence on providence, and people began wanting to individuate the major stages of the human adventure, perceived as part of a natural evolutionary plan and no longer of a creation resting entirely in the hands of God.

In England, Adam Ferguson's *History of Civil Society* (1767) established a three-part scheme of human evolution, divided into the savage, barbarian and civilized eras. This division was founded on ethnographic observations, and would reappear in the writings of many authors, up to Lewis Henry Morgan. In Germany we find Johann Herder, with his *Ideen zur Philosophie der Geschichte der Menschheit* (1784–1791), and Christopher Meiners, cited by Robert H. Lowie as the first true ethnologist. In 1785 Meiners published his works on the origin of society, *Grundriss der Geschichte der Menschheit*, a panorama illustrating human variability in time and space; it presents an authentic plan for ethnological research.

In Italy, Giambattista Vico demonstrated the principles of New Science. With his theory of courses and recourses, of cycles and refluxes, of evolutions and involutions, he sought the phases of the origins, and enunciated the law of the three states: the poetic (cosmogonies and mythology), heroic (the phase of historic-legendary epics), and finally, that of "intelligent human nature"—the stage of *ratio*, marked by equality and logical reasoning.

These were the first steps in the bold syntheses that would be attempted in the 19th century, in an effort to reconstruct human evolution, conceived according to a unilinear logic. Morgan would take up Ferguson's classification, while Auguste Comte, in turn, would take into account Vico's work.

CHAPTER II

The Great Journeys: Men Different from Us

Sixteenth-Century Europe: Breathing the Air of Freedom

The 16th century marks the greatest epistemological rupture in the history of Europe. There is no field that fails to undergo profound transformation in thought and action—from the linguistic field to the theological, from the scientific to the political. Luther's rebellion was one of the main causes (his famous Wittenberg theses became public in 1517)—not so much because of its religious consequences but because of the shock it effected throughout Europe, making nations and individuals abandon the blindness that always afflicts humanity: blindness in the presence of what is considered "obvious." Passive intellectual dependence on authorities and on pre-existing truths is the greatest obstacle to "research" in any area of life; it occurs spontaneously, with no recourse to force. In fact, it reflects a neuronic process analogous to that of communicating vessels; it does not arouse any resistance, since it functions on the basis of the principle of minimum effort. This principle is always valid for nearly all of humanity. I "see" what I expect to see—what I already know and, therefore, what I, in reality, recognize.

To become aware that we can follow different paths from the usual ones—paths new to thought and action—is nearly impossible. Still, when someone actually does so, the shock wave spreads everywhere—again, because of that identical principle of communicating vessels and minimum effort. This is just one more proof of the compact, global nature of every cultural "form"; consequently, it shows how wrong historians have been and still are, in considering the area of religion separate from the political one. It can also lead us to understand (to touch on a subject seemingly extraneous to our study, but which dramatically dominates our time) that economic theories and choices today are just as totalitarian as the religious ones of the past.

From the 16th to the 17th century, all centers of power were in competition with one another, not only for the conquest of territories, but above all for intellectual conquests. They vied with each other to possess the most precious volumes in their libraries, the most erudite scholars and the most important artists in their courts. A passion for Greek and Latin antiquity was the first fruit once men had torn down the wall supposedly marking the date of Christ's birth as the origin of the only true history.

This passion became one of the strongest stimuli for "research." "Research" is the concept—absolutely new at the time—that sums up and synthesizes the entire cultural pattern of the era. "Research" meant to spend all one's strength and all one's wealth in order to rediscover the texts of philosophers, poets, Greek and Latin historians, so that one could imitate them in producing one's own philosophy, one's own literature, one's own history. Here, obviously, "research" is focused on studying the formation of languages and one's *own* language, in the insatiable attempt to improve it through further "research" into the meaning of "rhetoric" and "style." Studying great historians such as Herodotus, Livy, Caesar, and Tacitus led to the idea of narrating the history of one's own country. Thus we see the flowering of hundreds of annals, chronicles, histories, diaries, biographies. Research, then, means the search for evidence, for sources, while widening the horizon of knowledge more and more. And when knowledge becomes the master of a man or an era, it is like a drug: one can never get enough of it (St. Paul had good reason in condemning it as *libido*).

The "search" for faraway lands, different ones, sprang forth from the same need, the same impulse. Just as ancient peoples, distant in time, become curiously interesting and near, so contemporary peoples, distant in space, become curiously interesting and near. The great geographic discoveries are thus born of the same passion:

"research." Indeed, they spring from the will of an individual, of one who thinks; only on a secondary level from the will of states. (As is commonly known, this applies to Christopher Columbus's voyage as well.)

The motor of Christian history in Europe has always been Rome, because the Pope is the head of the Christian empire, one which has simply taken the place of the Roman Empire. The usual vision of historians, who narrate history on the basis of a separation between the Eastern and Western empires, is obviously erroneous: only now, with the epistemological rupture of the 16th century, does the Western model totally differentiate itself from the Eastern one.

As we noted in the introduction, and as we shall have the occasion to recall during our journey through the history of anthropology, the global vision of events on the part of historians has always been warped by the primacy given to a "political" meter of judgment—obviously assumed to be the only correct one, as events presented themselves. Therefore, as regards the centuries passing from the advent of Christianity up to the end of the Pontifical State with the conquest of Rome, historians have always separated the sphere of sacred power of the Pope from the "earthly" one. Similarly, they have failed to become truly aware of the dominion exercised in all fields by monastic structures, present throughout Europe after the founding of numerous male and female orders. Unfortunately, history books never present a map of Europe showing the territorial and statistical distribution of monasteries, because this would be the only way to grasp their capillary "occupation" of the territory, and the immense cultural, economic, and social power they exercised.

Historians have failed to understand that the history of Christian Europe has been the history of the papacy and of monastic orders. Evident proof of this failure lies in the emphasis that they typically give to the "intolerable political invasiveness" of the Jesuits. But the Jesuits arrived at the end, when monastic power was already near exhaustion; and that is why it was easy to see a danger in the Jesuit order, and eliminate it. The fact that the Jesuits are the only order whose suppression was requested and obtained from the Pope, thus assumes an almost ridiculous tinge.

This premise is indispensable for understanding why Italy has always been at the center of European history, despite the scorn shown over the puniness of that nation's political clout (at least if we keep to what historians generally define as "political"). Men of power, on one side and the other, fought to conquer reigns in the name of Christ, but were obliged to send to Rome their most influential courtesans to ask the Pope to acknowledge their rights and victories. It was the Pope who decided which parts of conquered territories had to be attributed to Spain, which to France, and which to Portugal. Rome was the center of embassies of all the governments, and Rome was the principal seat of the Franciscans, Dominicans, Capuchins, and Jesuits: all religious orders, these, which placed their best scholars in the universities of Bologna, Padua, and Rome itself, and which enthusiastically embraced the ideal of evangelizing the lands to be discovered and conquered.

In Italy, though, there was no Reformation. The attempts at liberation, at a return to early Christianity, had been many. They were made much earlier, from 1100 till 1400, with the pauperistic movements, with Franciscanism, with popular preaching, but all had failed (see Ida Magli, *Gli uomini della penitenza*). The papal authority had reacted by becoming stronger and more coercive than ever. But precisely for this reason, liberty took other paths. Humanism, the Renaissance, spread into literary, linguistic, artistic and scientific "research." Aside from the seemingly servile dedications to the *Illustrissimi, Eccellentissimi Signori* on which they depended, the enthusiasts of research studied, wrote, measured, translated, traveled, and narrated. An extraordinary adventure of intelligence flamed up and spread from Italy to France, from France to Germany, from Germany to Spain, from Spain to England. All the scholars of the era recognized one another, exchanged news, and above all, abandoned themselves to the pleasures of knowledge and fantasy. If reflecting about Christian Europe was difficult and dangerous, the possibility of reflecting about the *other* emerged here.

An evasion, perhaps, but a hope as well.

The First Ethnographic Descriptions and Journey Accounts

The first anthropological description of "the natives" was published in 1512 (Paris: Henri Etienne): the *Nuova additio* to the *Chronicon* by Eusebius. Written in Latin, it tells of seven men led by canoe from America to Rouen; a detailed account is given of their clothing and weapons. Tattoos are mentioned; the men's hair is compared to horse manes, and the scarcity of body hair is emphasized. This latter fact would remain a theme of animated controversy, in discussions over the inferiority of the native Americans' virility.

Jacques Cartier briefly tells of customs pertinent to the tribes he encountered in a work significantly entitled *Brief récit avec particulières moeurs, langages et cérémonies des habitants fort délectables,* published in Paris in 1515. Travelers were now starting to collect observations of unequal value; highly varied information was collected into a growing number of compilations.

After Jacques Cartier for the North Americans and Alphonse Fonteneau for the Brazilians, the "king's cosmographer," André Thevet, composed an authentically ethnographic description of New World populaces. His observations on the Tupinambas are today considered an invaluable source of information, as are other accounts of the time, above all because they describe societies whose equilibrium had not yet been totally upset by the presence of Europeans.

Beginning in the first half of the 16th century, we see the first collections of accounts of the "great journeys," which little by little form a highly successful sort of "genre," halfway between literature and science. Of course, in order to perform notable works in this field, it was necessary to possess not only the capacity to make a patient, careful elaboration of data from the most varied sources, but also a vast knowledge of numerous languages, and a profound basic erudition. Together with the missionaries' determination, these characteristics—in an era when persons who dedicated themselves to study were almost exclusively members of religious orders—explain the very marked presence of Franciscans, Dominicans and Jesuits among the writers of journey accounts. They also explain why the great majority of these men were Italian in origin or—though coming from other nations—Italian in their intellectual formation.

Among the collections of journey accounts, perhaps the best work is by Giambattista Ramusio, an extremely learned man, secretary to the Council of Ten in the Republic of Venice, and custodian of the public library of St. Mark. In the three volumes of his *Raccolta di navigazioni e di viaggi* we find some of the most important accounts written or reported by travelers and explorers, of all times and countries. What is even more important, the accounts are not merely juxtaposed, but compared to one another.

However, premises of mythological or theological origin were still mixed continually with factual documents. Deforming images would last for an extremely long period and raise useless questions for scholars: the teratological theme, the theme of the Good Savage, supported by a great number of missionaries (it was through this myth that the values of "civilization" began to be questioned); and, linked to this, the mythological themes of the Fountain of Youth, Eldorado, and the Golden Age.

Among 16th-century travelers, the most important historiographer was Pietro Martire d'Anghiera (1469–1536), who lived at the court of Spain. In his *Decades de Orbe Novo*, first published in complete form in 1516, he narrates in detail the 34-year-old history of overseas discoveries, and the conquests of the western hemisphere beginning with Columbus's first enterprise. Pietro Martire's data is precious and reliable, for he succeeded in being present at the assemblies of the Council of the Indies, read correspondence from abroad, and was personally acquainted with Amerigo Vespucci, John Cabot and other illustrious navigators. Above all, he was an intimate friend of Christopher Columbus.

One of the most eminent travelers of the time was Marco da Nizza (dates of birth and death unknown), a Franciscan sent to America to preach the gospel to Amerindian tribes in northern Mexico. In 1539 he found himself in the town of Culnacán, on the border of lands ruled by the Spanish at the time. He collected the impressions he had seen and heard in an account praising the lands he had visited; his reports exalted the already fervid minds of conquistadores and adventurers, so acutely that men ended up believing they had found Eldorado. The expedition by Vázquez Coronado in 1540 reduced the wealth that Brother Marco boasted of to more modest proportions. The Franciscan does deserve recognition, at any rate, for having first made known the region of Sonora, where in accordance with his accounts, the gold attracting hordes of seekers was finally found.

Girolamo Benzoni (1519, d. perhaps after 1566), left for America in 1542. He lived there for 14 years, journeying over vast areas of territory and observing people, customs and religions. His travel account, *Historia del Mundo Nuovo* (1565), became famous in Europe.

Filippo Sassetti (1540–1588), a noble Florentine, was in Lisbon in 1577 on business. There he was given the chance to travel to the East Indies in the honored and lucrative position of superintendent of pepper supplies, which were to be carried to Lisbon and Cádiz. After a dangerous voyage he arrived in India, where he remained for a number of years, carefully observing the customs and habits of the place, and finding interest in its history, laws and religious institutions. He was the first European who perceived the importance of Sanskrit, and that language's kinship to the Latin and Germanic languages. He died in Goa in 1588; his studies have come down to us through the *Lettere di Spagna, Portogallo e Indie*, and the collected *Lettere* published in Florence in 1855 (some of which had not been published until that date).

Francesco Carletti (1573?–1636), from a Florentine family of merchants, set off for America from Seville with his father and a shipload of slaves, bought on the Cape Verde Islands. After a long period of sailing they stopped in Japan, and then reached China, where they remained for several years. Having grown wealthy through trade, Carletti decided to return to Europe in 1602 with a load of precious goods and all of his personal belongings, on a Portuguese ship, but off the Island of St. Helena, the Dutch, at war with Portugal, took possession of the ship and all its riches. After returning to Florence, Carletti became the first traveler to acquaint Italy with cocoa and chocolate. He narrates his wanderings in *Ragionamenti sopra le cose da lui vedute nei suoi viaggi sì delle Indie Occidentali e Orientali come d'altri paesi,* published in Florence in 1701.

Pietro Della Valle (1586–1652) was born in Rome of a noble family. His voyages were different from those undertaken by most private citizens like himself, for he took with him a large following of servants, and traveled all over the Orient like a great lord, welcomed everywhere by princes and sovereigns. During the course of his wanderings he married an aristocratic Indian lady, and then continued his travels with her to Persia. After she died he carried her body along with him in a coffin for four years, until he reached Rome, where he buried her in the splendid family tomb. He died in Rome in 1652, after publishing the account of his voyage to Turkey; whereas the accounts of his travels in Persia and India came to light several years later, thanks to his children.

An acute observer, he spoke and wrote Turkic, Persian, and Arabic, and had some knowledge of Coptic and Chaldean. He utilized his out-of-the-ordinary knowledge of oriental languages in order to understand the customs of the places he visited. He burrowed into the second pyramid, removing two mummies from it along with other objects. During his travels in Mesopotamia he was struck by cuneiform writing. He presented several characters of this and, while declaring himself unable to understand it, guessed that it was meant to be read from left to right. His travel accounts became famous and were translated into many languages.

Francesco Giuseppe Bressani (1612–1672) became a Jesuit in 1627, and asked to be sent to the American mission. In 1642 he was in Quebec, and two years later, amidst the Hurons. During this mission he was taken prisoner by the Iroquois, who believed he was French; they subjected him to torture and mistreatment of all kinds. Finally he was sold to the Dutch, and sent back to France in 1644. The year after he chose to return to his mission among the Hurons, who welcomed him back favorably; in 1649, given his poor health, he was called back home. He died in Florence in 1672. The account of his mission, published in Macerata in 1653, draws a detailed picture of the customs of the Hurons and other Amerindians which at that time occupied upper and lower Canada, and the regions near New France.

Around the World with Francesco Gemelli Careri

In 1686, Francesco Gemelli Careri (1651; d. ?) visited Italy, and then traveled through France, England and Holland. He passed through Germany and arrived in Vienna, where he offered his services to the emperor in the war against the Turks. In June 1693, having boarded ship at Malta, he sailed for Egypt, saw Alexandria and Cairo and described the surrounding lands, studying their customs and government. He then went on to Persia, where he visited the ruins at Persepolis and, although lacking in the archeological and linguistic knowledge necessary for travelers, described with careful observation and a fair degree of exactness the ruins of Persepolis. From Persia he passed into the Indies; he reached Goa and finally, the Empire of the Great Mogul, about which he presents a great deal of interesting particulars. From India he traveled to China, landing at Canton. His arrival coincided with the moment of the Catholic controversy over the "Chinese rites," so that he was viewed suspiciously by the Jesuit and Franciscan missionaries, who thought he was an emissary from Rome come to look into matters. From China he sailed to the Philippines, after giving a precise description of many Chinese customs, and the Great Wall. From Manila he left on a Spanish galleon for the Americas; he landed at Acapulco.

Careri draws a sorry picture of the Mexico of his time, describing the slavery there, disease, wars, and painful economic conditions to which it had been reduced by Spanish rule. His attention was riveted by the great ruins of the Teotihuacan pyramids, which he accurately described. Boarding ship later on for Vera Cruz, he returned to Europe, landing at Naples in 1698, after completing a journey around the world in five years, five months and 20 days. Gemelli Careri's account was published in 1701 and translated into a number of languages.

Francesco Orazio da Pennabilli (1680–1747) entered the order of Capuchin Friars, and in 1719 left on a mission to Tibet. For 5 years, together with 12 brothers of the Order, he preached the Gospel; because of disease and the hardships of climate he was forced to return to Europe in 1735. He left again for Tibet in 1739, bearing gifts for the Tibetan princes and for the Dalai Lama, from whom he obtained permission to freely carry on his missionary activity. In those years he became profoundly proficient in the Tibetan language and, under his direction, in 1738 the first Tibetan letters were molded in metal; they were used by the Propaganda Fide Congregation to print books in that language. He died in

1747 in a city of Nepal. His *Relazione del principio e stato presente della missione nel vasto regno del Tibet e regni confinanti raccomandata allo zelo dei Padri Cappuccini della Marca* was printed in Rome in 1742.

Matteo Ricci's "Adaptation"

An area in which missionary work opened up possibilities for intercultural relations and presented new issues which were perceived in the West as well (however, to a lesser degree), was Asia Minor. This is not the place to write a history of the influence that the missions had in the problems that came up during this period—from strictly philosophical to linguistic, political and religious ones. But as regards China, we cannot help but recall the importance of Matteo Ricci (1552–1610) and Prospero Intorcetta (1626–1696).

Matteo Ricci (whose works were published by Pietro Tacchi-Venturi in 1911–13) not only possessed a profound knowledge of the Chinese religious world, but also defended the thesis known as "adaptation," which was important for its historico-religious meanings and for the new attitudes shown by Christians toward other religions. This thesis assumed there was a certain "natural goodness" in non–Christian customs and morals, and therefore foresaw the possibility of adapting some aspects of Christianity to local customs in order to favor evangelization. In reality, Ricci did not renounce the assumption of Christianity's absolute truth, and his method was only a means for spreading his religion; but at the same time, he did recognize the "original purity of the Religion of Nature." Thus a new disposability on the part of Christians in their relations with other cultural universes began to find concrete form, and people began to realize the importance of an adequate linguistic and ethnological preparation for missionaries. Such preparation necessarily meant progress in anthropological and cultural studies.

The Jesuit Prospero Intorcetta, instead, was important for introducing the first translation of Confucius to Europe; whereas the information coming from the missionaries in India was much less influential in European culture. For example, the writings of the Jesuit Roberto De Nobili (1577–1656) found no relevant echo;

nor did those of that other Jesuit, Giacomo Fenicio (1558–1632); nonetheless, both had a profound knowledge of Indian religious life. De Nobili in particular had applied the methods of "adaptation" to India, and had thus recognized the need to show great respect toward its ancient cultural traditions.

The usefulness of these sources, at any rate, was lessened by the fact that any news of an historical or religious character furnished by the missionaries was submerged and nearly suffocated by theological and power-linked diatribes coinciding with the so-called "question of Chinese and Malabar rites," which we hinted at earlier. Many theologians, in fact, were contrary to the method of "accommodation," since they believed it to be a confused mixture of Christianity with other religions, and therefore, in some way, a renunciation of pure evangelization. In this case, it is clear that the missionaries realized the need to find a system of "acculturation" which would be the least traumatic as possible, but the central authorities were unable to harvest good fruit from this experience.

CHAPTER III

The Seventeenth and Eighteenth Centuries

Races, Climate, and Relations Among Religions

The contribution of the 17th century and that of the late 18th century to ethnological knowledge reveal important differences. The 1600s were not really open to overseas realities; European culture during that century remained concentrated on itself; one might even say that it drew from faraway societies only a pretext for exoticism. The 1700s changed the perspective. People began wondering about the meaning of non–Western cultures; cosmopolitanism grew, and there seemed to be a passage from exoticism to an authentic form of humanism.

Travel accounts of the 17th century, however, had an unmistakably ethnological value. Jean Mocquet replaced André Thevet; in 1616 he wrote a travelogue, *Voyages en Afrique, Asie, Indes Orientales et Occidentales*, in which prejudice often surpasses objective description. The year 1600 saw the rise of the "climate" theory, found mainly in Father Gabriel Sagard, and Father Claude d'Abbéville, who in his *Histoire de la Mission en Isle de Maragnon* (1614) wrote a chapter entitled "Du Naturel et de l'esprit des Maragnons," affirming that "philosophy teaches, and experience well demonstrates, that a good temperature greatly benefits not only the body, but the intellect as well, and man's entire nature." The idea of the natural environment's influence on the cultural environment is foreshadowed here. This would later be the fundamental element in Montesquieu's demonstration, and the premise for an *ethnopsychology*.

This period also witnessed an enormous increase in documentation from the various missionary orders, especially the Jesuits: first in South America, and later in the Far East. The severe administration of the Jesuits demanded regular reports from each missionary present in missionary lands. Thus it was possible to form immense archives containing information which, though unequal in value, always presents elements of interest; for a number of populaces it constitutes the first written ethnological testimony.

From the end of the 16th century to 1700, theological debate grew regarding the origin of races, the theory of climatic influence, and the problem of Christianity's relation to other religions.

By the end of the 16th century, Jean Bodin (1529–1596) had included among his political and juridical treatises an important essay, *Heptaplomeres* (composed around 1593). It centered on the problem of the relation among the different religions, and explicitly inaugurated the thesis of a "natural religion" which was universally accepted, and reflected in Moses' Ten Commandments. This thesis of a minimum natural religion, seen to subsist in non–Christian religions and to foreshadow the primitive Revelation, was reached from various directions during the course of the 17th century. Gerardus Johannis Vossius (1577–1649), in his *De Theologia Gentili et Physiologia christiana seu de origine ad progressu idolatriae ad veterum gesta ac rerum naturam reductae* (1641), takes up the thesis of "degeneration" (according to which the pagan religions reveal the remaining traces of a revealed religion). In so doing, he intends to reach Bodin's aim, assuming an attitude of tolerance and understanding toward the non–Christian world. According to Vossius, the great Greek and Roman gods are identifiable with persons from the Old Testament; this fact presupposes an original, universal diffusion of the Scriptures, destroyed in part by the deceitful action of the ancient pagan priesthood.

Between the second half of the 17th and the first half of the 18th centuries, data was acquired which would become fundamental in the development of ethnological history, even in its religious aspects. First of all we should recall the great flow of information from missionaries in North America, the Jesuits in particular. Of course, their accounts prevalently reflect a lively preoccupation with the mission, with evangelization; moreover, they often pertain to the difficult, violent polemics of power. At the same time, they do present interesting news concerning the world of the northern Amerindians, prior to its disintegration due to colonialism.

In the 17th century the Jesuits' accounts—especially those relative to Canada—are devoid of any idealized interpretation of native American societies (such as that of the "good savage"); on the contrary, they frequently denounce the "superstitions," malignity, craftiness and immorality of the natives. However, even while adapting the theological premise that such peoples could become "civil" if they were "saved" by the Christian Revelation, some missionary writers assume particular importance: both because (in some cases) they present a native world of "natural goodness" or "ingenuousness" predisposed to good, and because they propose and resolve the serious fundamental problem of the relation between the primitive or "savage" religions, and revealed Christianity.

These ideas, which were to appear in mature form in the works of Joseph François Lafiteau, have important precedents, among which are the writings of Marc Lescarbot (b. 1590 ca.). A lawyer in the Paris Parliament, he followed Baron Poutrincourt to Canada and, after returning to France, published *Histoire de la Nouvelle France* (1609), and later, three *Relations* (1610–1612). Particularly in the *Relations*, he declares himself an adversary of the Jesuit settlers; at any rate, his *Histoire* contains an early attempt to establish a parallel—taken up repeatedly by later scholars—between the customs of the "ancients" and those of the American "savages" (the sixth book of the *Histoire* is dedicated to the "customs ... of the western natives of New France, as compared to those of the ancient peoples").

Montesquieu (1689–1755), in turn, contributed to the debate by affirming that man constructs himself and his time according to a complex web of factors, but on an autonomous level (which excludes transcendence); in a concrete historical and environmental reality, sufficient to explain the various societies and their growth. One of Montesquieu's main intentions is to demonstrate the constant influence of climate—of geophysical activity—on the characters and attitudes of peoples. In *L'Esprit des Lois* (1748), the whole of Book XVIII is dedicated to the laws governing man's relationship to the nature of the land, even though this deterministic premise appears to be attenuated by the importance given to the man-made landscape. Religions are considered in their variability, in relation to the various histories and factors determining the traits of nations, according to a general rule touching on religions and, indeed, on all manifestations of the spirit. The particular climate and character of the Eastern populaces, for example, explains the immutability of their religious structures:

> The belief in metempsychosis is made for the climate of the Indies. The excessive heat burns all the countryside, and only a small number of cattle manages to find nourishment; there is always danger they will be lacking for the work of plowing, while oxen only multiply in mediocre numbers, and are subject to many diseases. A religious law which can preserve them is therefore highly convenient to the order of the country.

Analogously, Montesquieu thinks that the Athenian custom, according to which it was right to honor the gods more with small gifts than with great sacrifices, depended on the sterility of the territory and the limited availability of goods to sacrifice. Moreover, he thought it was difficult for a religion to be transferred from its original territory and formation to another territory, precisely because of the direct link between the religious reality and the environment. Each religion is an historical formation, and so the passage of a religion from one country to another brings serious problems, and causes phenomena that (to use a modern expression) are culturally "disintegrative."

These interpretative perspectives naturally interested the liveliest thinkers of the Enlightenment and the writers of the *Encyclopedia*. Voltaire himself considered Montesquieu as one who had restored dignity to mankind.

The Calvinist theologian, Pierre Jurieu (1637–1713), moving within the realm of the history of religions, took up the thesis of "condescendence," which had already appeared in the work of the Anglican theologian, John Spencer: God conceded to Jews the right to contaminate themselves by accepting rites of non-revealed origin; therefore, a paganism exists independently of Judaism, tolerated by God for the sake of salvation. An important theory, this one of Spencer's. As several scholars have pointed out, it laid the foundations for the science of religion in the sense that, in order to support his premises, he presupposed relations between Judaic rites and those of other Semitic peoples. Jurieu reveals Spencer's influence in his work, *Histoire critique des dogmes et des cultes bons et mauvais qui ont été dans l'Eglise depuis Adam jusqu'à Jésus-Christ* (1704). Here he traces "idolatrous" elements even in the Old Testament, explaining their presence by saying they are tolerated by God. Such an explanation also finds force in the theory of "allegorism," according to which the ancient sages hid natural and moral science under myths; and the theory of "degeneration," according to which polytheism is a phenomenon posterior to the monotheism which was revealed before the Flood.

The Jesuit missionary Joseph François Lafiteau (1670–1740) bases his work *Moeurs des Sauvages Amériquains* (1724) on his own ethnological observations of the Canadian Indians, and on research done by his religious companion, Jean Garnier, who had lived in the Canadian missions for 60 years, learning some of the native languages. Lafiteau concludes by asserting the relevance of primitive cultural forms to explanations given by classical cultures. In particular, he thinks he can make out among ethnological data certain elements which are common to all peoples, since they conform to human nature, and find their origin in the revelation made by God to Adam. (His thought thus reflects the theory of the involution of an original monotheistic idea; this theory was to be taken up again later in more explicit form by Wilhelm Schmidt.)

Father Lafiteau was a careful gatherer of data, both as a direct observer of the natives and through a reelaboration of those historical sources written by other missionaries, which were available to him. Even when he assumes moralistic attitudes regarding given data, or tries to discover in them traces of the revealed universal religion, or parallels with the biblical tradition, his success in making classifications and organizing materials reflects one of the earliest serious efforts to understand the great variety and customs of the so-called savages. The work is accompanied by drawings—often naive ones, but useful in integrating Lafiteau's design, by presenting to Westerners human groups living according to their own norms and habits; groups which vary from territory to territory, each in accordance with its own history. The resulting picture allowed scholars to overcome the former image of an undetermined, amorphous "wildness." In his second volume, for example, on the basis of the Jesuits' accounts, Lafiteau stops to consider the "general festival of the dead," proper to most of the "savage nations"; but at the same time, he intelligently indicates the differences in its development within the various ethnic groups. And he graphically depicts the ten-year festival of the dead among the Hurons and Iroquois.

Lafiteau's theses (which present profound analogies with those later proposed by scholars of the historico-cultural current), can be summed up in the principle according to which the basis (which we could also call phenomenological traits or structures) of religions among the American savages is identical to that of the religions of the barbarians who occupied Greece and spread to Africa, and to the religions of all the peoples giving origin to "pagan mythology." It is on these grounds that one can deduce a common origin for all religions: i.e., the Revelation made to the early forefathers after the Fall. The present multiplicity of religions—the coexistence of a true revealed religion (the Christian) alongside numerous other religions cannot be explained without hypothesizing a "degeneration." The first revealed religion was deformed following the many vicissitudes of human history, such as allegorization, the attribution of a divine nature to Adam and Eve, diabolical disguising, etc.

The Jesuit François Xavier de Charlevoix (1682–1761), in highly important works such as *Histoire et description générale de la Nouvelle-France* (1744) and *Histoire du Japon* (1754), presents a synthesis of ethno-religious data regarding Canada and other mission lands. He puts forward a hypothesis regarding the origin of the Canadian Indians and their religions. He thought the Canadians had come from the Orient before or after the Flood. Charlevoix then claims the necessity of comparative linguistics to ascertain the origins of those peoples.

The vision of humanity thus widened considerably in the 18th century. This vision progressively embraced the "eccentric" peoples, discovering aspects of humanity whose existence had never been suspected till then; while Orientalism—and very soon, what would become Indianism—revealed vanished civilizations which were once mighty and beautiful, though owing nothing to the West! This vision expanded not only in space, but in time as well. Here the contribution of archeology was decisive, introducing—albeit in gradual stages—a radical disruption in the European conceptions of the origin of human culture. The search for everything preceding present reality was projected so far into the remote past that it surpassed the historical dimension and came to constitute prehistory.

By the beginning of the 18th century, Joseph de Jussieu and Father Lafiteau had established the first parallels between the stone weapons used by primitives of the time, and prehistoric ones. This marked the start of a long-lived controversy between individual researchers, who were freer from the influence of the various hierarchies, and those representing the academies and other official organizations. The former tended to demonstrate the antiquity of humanity before the Flood, while the latter observed theories respecting the authority of the Scriptures, including the periods of duration established on the basis of the Bible. Moreover, prehistoric evidence from tombs, especially skeletons which were larger than the average anthropometric standard, seemed to demonstrate the historical value of the biblical story of the universal flood, and the era of Giants preceding it. Thus such interpretations of evidence from tombs influenced the philosophic-religious model of the "giants" and the "big beasts" of the forests, which continued to have a place in European culture during the entire 18th century.

At the same time, another movement began to make way: one tending to place humanity once again in a geological framework. Aristotle had already placed it there, but this aspect of his work had been forgotten for more than 2000 years. In 1735 the Swedish naturalist Linnaeus (1707–1778) classified the human animal according to a division of six great "races": "savage" man, American man, Asiatic man, African man, European man and teratological man (*monstruosus*)—this last group including all the deviant types described with such deep conviction, beginning in the Middle Ages: giants, pygmies, wolf-men, men with tails, etc.

Thus began a great adventure: humanity was discovering its own duration in time.

The Great Ocean Voyages and the Work of the "Observateurs de l'Homme"

In the 18th and 19th centuries, an intermediate period marked the passage from an archaic society to a modern one. The threshold of this nearly 30-year period saw the rise of the three terms of "ethnology," "ethnography," and "anthropology," used to qualify, first of all, the history of peoples' progress toward civilization, then the classification of races according to their different traits. In this sense, "ethnology" tended to assume a raciological meaning; while "ethnography" tended to indicate an ethnic inventory centered around the linguistic characteristics of peoples. "Anthropology," instead, was used by Johann F. Blumenbach in 1795 to qualify the natural history of man (in the "Letter of Dedication" presented as a foreword to the third edition of his *De generis humani varietate nativa*); later the term was vulgarized, coming to indicate the science of mankind in general. Finally, the word "folklore" is more recent. It was coined in England by William J. Thoms in 1846.

Ethnological research has been carried out by two kinds of scholars: those in the field and those working theoretically. The former included travelers—explorers in particular—whose theoretical knowledge was sometimes only rudimental, but who were relatively open to an understanding of the *other*. The theoreticians, instead, were learned men of widely varying professional backgrounds, but united by the same will—not yet explicitly formulated—to define what would later be called the "total man."

These "ideologues" aimed at gaining a global vision; in many respects, they resembled modern ethnologists. The importance of the "ideologues" in the history of ideas in France, and the rest of Europe, is being more and more widely acknowledged today, but their contribution to the history of ethnology has not yet been sufficiently highlighted. Moreover, the "philosophes" were able to base their work, not only on abstract speculation, but above all on a type of documentation that we might call ethnographical: the body of documentation accumulated by travelers.

Among the latter, we should mention in particular the discoverers of the ocean archipelagos, citing the accounts of James

Cook, George Forster, Sydney Parkinson, and Louis-Antoine de Bougainville. These were authentic humanists: spirits open to an understanding of "different" civilizations, and eager to document at least the most visible aspects of the societies in which they spent a few days or weeks. In Cook's tales of navigation, which go from 1768 to 1780, we find a great deal of curiosity and even a certain degree of cordiality toward the natives—the Maori, Tahitians, Fijians, and Indians of Vancouver—but there is no idealization; indeed, a taste for realism stands out in contrast to the myth of the good savage.

The position of Louis-Antoine de Bougainville, a military man and scientist, went beyond that of other travelers. He was called to membership in the society of the "Observateurs de l'Homme" by Louis-François Jauffret, in the function of geographer, together with Nicolas Baudin, François Levaillant and others. In 1767, on board the frigate *Boudeuse*, he undertook a voyage of scientific exploration in the Pacific Ocean, which he crossed from east to west. After his voyage around the world, he brought back Aotourou, a young Tahitian native. During the expedition itself, Bougainville began a series of studies on the Tahitian youth, attempting at the same time to familiarize him with European customs. Once back home, in Paris, he hoped to arouse systematic interests and rigorous research, but he was soon disappointed. Certainly, the people's wish to see the "savage" was quite lively at first; but—as Bougainville noted sadly—this was a sterile kind of curiosity "which serves only to give false ideas to men whose nature it is to ridicule, who have never been outside the capital, who never go below the surface of anything and who, prey to errors of every type, see things only in the light of their prejudices, and yet pronounce severe sentences without appeal" (*Voyage autour du monde*, 1771). His *Voyage autour du monde* also attracted attention to the Papuasians, and gave Diderot inspiration for his famous *Supplément au Voyage de Bougainville* (1772).

One of Bougainville's companions, the naturalist Philibert Commerson, decided to publicize news of the discovery of Tahiti, nicknamed Nouvelle Cythère. In a note about the island appearing in November 1789 in the *Mercure de France*, Commerson drew a bright picture of those peoples "born under the most beautiful sky, nourished by the fruits of a land which is fecund even without being cultivated, governed by family fathers rather than by kings." It was the only corner of the earth where people lived without vices, without prejudices, without needs, without discord. The dispute over Tahiti began then, even before the appearance of Bougainville's *Voyage*. Bougainville himself appears much more cautious than Commerson, and the image that he gives of Tahitians, together with testimony from Samuel Wallis and Cook, would later serve to support Buffon's refusal of the mythical illusion. It would almost seem that the image of the Tahitians crystallized two opposing visions of the world and savage man. Their goodness and felicity do not seem so evident to everyone. These qualities are found as examples in Tahiti only by those who, sensitive to the misery of "social" man, found in that island Eden the model for a free, happy life within a "natural" society.

In the course of this intermediate period which so greatly renewed ideas and people, one spiritual "family" assumed particular importance: the Ideologues. It was in the wake of ideas created by the Ideologues that the Société des Observateurs de l'Homme was formed; it would last only six years, from 1799 to 1805. In a perspective so vast that one cannot truly calculate its originality and anticipation with respect to the times, this society was created to unite all the researchers who found in humanity their new "object" of study. The society was led by a permanent secretary, an erudite man, one of the most important turn-of-the-century figures: François Jauffret (1770–1840). This researcher, a zoologist and "philosophe," was probably a professor of the first regular course of ethnography that had ever existed in France and, perhaps, in the world; first in Paris, then in Marseilles, he taught students about exotic populaces. Jauffret was also the first scholar to elaborate a project for an ethnographic museum; in 1803, in fact, he is said to have published a *Mémoire pour l'établissement d'un Muséum anthropologique* (though the text cannot be found today).

The Société des Observateurs de l'Homme had the merit of conceiving a well-coordinated, systematically-organized program of research in view of Captain Baudin's explorations in Oceania. Instructions were issued by a commission which included Georges Cuvier, Joseph-Marie Degérando and Jauffret. Degérando was interested in the methodological aspects of research on exotic societies, and drew up a questionnaire, *Considérations sur les diverses méthodes à suivre dans l'observation des peuples sauvages*—the first work of its kind. The clear direction in which the Ideologues were heading can be seen by their intention to correlate the most diverse phenomena in which humanity had been involved: the environment, biology, physiology, psychology, etc. It was in the 18th century, too, that the different variables or determining factors of the human being began to take shape. The movement that tended to place the human species in its correct niche was now being affirmed with less and less timidity.

The new science of linguistics also began to form in this period. Constantin-François de Volney (1757–1820), the precursor of geographic history and human geography, had acutely foreseen the importance of this new discipline. However, his expectations regarding it were probably too audacious. De Volney conceived of linguistics as a philosophy of language, giving to "philosophy" the sense of a global study, including both the problem of origins and research on the laws of evolution, with the conviction that through the study of languages, one could proceed far back into the human past. Indeed, de Volney thought it was possible to find the primitive nucleus giving rise to all languages; he even hoped to discover through an analysis of the elements constituting this fundamental nucleus the very mechanism of the formation of language, the first invention and the distinctive sign of culture (*Discours sur l'étude philosophique des langues*, 1819).

Scholars of the period were not only interested in language in the abstract, but in concrete languages as well. Travelers wrote down the new languages with which they came into contact, even though no professional linguist as yet existed. Alexander von Humboldt (1769–1859), for example, was a naturalist. The most interesting part of his great ethnological work is found in *Essai politique sur le Royaume de la Nouvelle-Espagne*, of 1811, and in *Vues des Cordillères et monuments des Peuples indigènes de l'Amérique*, of 1816. Humboldt possessed a new consciousness of the need for "mental deconditioning" in order to approach any different civilization; he tried to define as distinctly as possible the relations between societies and the environment; and he also investigated the economical and political aspects of Amerindian cultures.

Charles de Brosses, in turn, together with Antoine Court de Gébelin, had dreamed of compiling a comparative dictionary of all known languages. Jauffret praised him, together with William Warburton, as a philosopher of language, especially since he emphasized the centrality of the imitative function in the elaboration of hieroglyphics. In his *Histoire des navigations aux terres australes* (1756), Charles de Brosses introduces the terms "Australia" and "Polynesia," and draws a picture of oceanic cultures, comprising one of the least-known exotic worlds of the time. He then delimits the space still remaining to be explored: "I call austral lands all those which are situated beyond the three southern points of the known world, in Africa, Asia and America: that is, beyond the Cape of Good Hope, the Moluccan and Celebes Islands, and the Strait of Magellan"; he continued by affirming that there must be, in such a vast part of the world, some immense continent of solid earth situated south of Asia, capable of keeping the globe in equilibrium during its rotation, as well as serving as counterweight to the mass of northern Asia. Besides the economic interest offered by trade that might be carried out with the inhabitants of this continent, he was intrigued by the image of such numerous peoples differing from one another—and above all, from "us"—in appearance, customs, habits, ideas, forms of worship. For de Brosses, the term "savages" had a positive connotation on an epistemological level. It is within this perspective that the essay, *Dieux Fétiches*, acquires methodological and cultural value.

With respect to scholars who had previously studied matters which could now be defined as "ethnological," de Brosses doubtlessly made a great deal of headway. Involved in research on mythology, he did not see in myth the fruit of error and superstition; rather, he criticized the ancient Greeks, responsible for mixtures and layering which have made the interpretation of ancient myths so much more complicated. Despite this situation of mythology, added de Brosses, scholars of the time had finally found the key to the true history of the earliest peoples, their opinions and memories. Precisely in studying this "real history," he became aware of the existence, in various spatial and temporal areas, of a relatively constant structure concerning a certain type of religious belief and worship which he calls "fetishism." He noted that this structure is present among ancient and modern populaces, and therefore the problem facing him was the fetishistic structure as such. The savage populaces appeared to him as a precious instrument for understanding civilized populations in their original state. His true aim was thus not so much to study given "primitive" peoples, but rather to enucleate structures of thought and life which were common to various human societies. This objective could not be reached except through the use of systematic comparison. After explaining the "fetishism" of nations of my time—he says—I will compare it to that of ancient peoples; and this parallel, leading us naturally to judge that the same actions have the same principle, will show us quite clearly that all of these peoples had, in fetishism, the same manner of thinking, since their manner of acting, which was its logical consequence, has been the same (*Du culte des dieux fétiches, ou Parallèle de l'ancienne religion de l'Egypte avec la religion actuelle de Nigritie*, 1760).

Abbot Nicolas Sylvestre Bergier studied fetishism as well. After doing research on the primitive elements of languages, he dedicated himself to the study of primitive religions. His theory, based on careful documentation and expressed in a calm, balanced tone, precedes Edward Burnett Tylor's animistic theory by about a century. In *L'origine des dieux du paganisme* (1767), he dates fetishism and star worship back to an "infantile mentality," leading peoples to assign the presence of spirits and geni to things, to nature.

Like Voltaire and de Brosses, Abbot Guillaume François Raynal, on his part, utilizes the notion of fetishism to indicate a belief in divine forces connected to nature in various ways. In his famous pages contrasting savage man to civilized man, Raynal demonstrates a perfect awareness that his proper task was not to exalt savage man as such, but to promote in "civilized" man a critical consciousness of the disorder and vices afflicting the over-praised civilization of Europe, by way of an unprejudiced analysis of certain non-negative aspects of primitive life. Indeed, at the end of the chapter entitled "Comparison between civilized peoples and savage peoples," he writes in *Histoire philosophique et politique des établissements du Commerce des Européens dans les Deux Indes* (1774):

> Civilized peoples, this parallel is doubtlessly painful for you, but you can never feel too strongly the calamities under whose burden you moan. The more this sensation is painful to you, the more capable it will be of making you attentive to the true causes of your ills. Perhaps you will finally come to convince yourselves

that they find their origin in the disorderly nature of your opinions, in the vices of your political constitutions, in the bizarre laws by which natural laws are continually offended.

Jean-Nicolas Démeunier, a scholar showing great affinity with the Ideologues and the "Observateurs," acutely emphasized the two needs of observational and comparative research. He complained that, after accumulating such a great number of books about mankind, researchers had not yet attempted to compare the customs, habits, and laws of different peoples. Such an investigation should be taken up as soon as possible: "We know nearly all the nations, civilized and savage; now the time has come to compare them. Up till now writers have not presented the customs of 'Others' except from a bizarre or ridiculous point of view, out of the old defect of believing that our customs and our laws must serve as a model for all the laws of the world" (*Esprit des usages et des coutumes des différents peuples ou observations tirées des voyageurs et des historiens*, 1776).

Such observations would remain valid as time passed.

The Dispute Over the "New World"

The thesis of the "weakness" or "immaturity" of the Americas originated with Buffon around the middle of the 18th century. According to Buffon, all the animals of the New World are smaller and weaker than those of the Old World. The important animals have become smaller and less appetizing, meaning that the atmosphere, the American environment, is hostile to the development of animals. Buffon proceeds further in this direction by extending the parallel from observations concerning quadrupeds, to all of living nature. The savage is weak; his genitalia are small; he has neither body hair nor beard, and feels no ardor toward women. He is less strong than the European, and is devoid of any liveliness or activity of the soul. If you take away his hunger and thirst you also destroy the activating principle of all his movements; he will remain stupidly at rest, standing or lying down, for days at a time.

The singular link between the impotence of the savage and the absence of great ferocious beasts seems to suggest another idea to Buffon. The savage is cold; the serpent is cold; cold-blooded animals are cold. America is crawling with reptiles and insects, and they are often gigantic. This is due to the quality of the soil, the condition of the sky, the degree of heat and humidity, the quantity of running and stagnant water, the extension of the forests; and above all, to the brutal state in which nature lies. The marshy aspect of the landscape is therefore of utmost importance. Rousseau had praised the sexual moderation of the savage as proof of his placid obedience to the natural instinct, never spurred on by a lurid imagination, by female tricks, or by absurd jealousies. On the contrary, in Buffon's opinion, the American man is worse off than other animals because of his sexual frigidity. Moreover, a kind of vicious circle is created between the humidity of the American soil and the apathetic character of the natives: They do not work, do not transform the land, which could be freed of putrefaction only by the labor of man.

Theories regarding the relation between the humidity of the environment and the teeming insects and serpents mentioned by Buffon were probably due to the long disputes that went on during the 17th century regarding the spontaneous generation of worms and vipers from rotting bodies and wetlands. Another premise for Buffon's argument is that whatever is stable, fixed, invariable, is superior to what varies; therefore whatever is large, being less variable than what is small, is less valuable. The varieties of a species are explained exclusively as degenerative forms of a prototype. Except for a few major species such as man, the elephant, the rhinoceros, the hippopotamus, the tiger and the lion, which proudly stand by themselves, animal species mix among each other and form degenerate groups. The assumption that the invariable is superior to the mutable closes Buffon off from any historical type of perspective, and leads him to classify living beings according to their volume, given that the large is more stable than the small. Such a theory belonged to the ambit of that mythical vision of the whale and the elephant which had characterized the Middle Ages. According to Buffon, nature is not subject to the law of "progress." At its best, nature is in a state of immobility; at its worst, in one of degeneration. By intervening in nature, by searching for progress in spite of it, man himself is the cause of degeneration in nature; indeed, the ferocious beasts, being near to nature and free from the action of man, are less subject to degenerative variations. This idea took up a theme dear to Michel Eyquem de Montaigne: the superiority of wild fruit to cultivated fruit; and it gave a "scientific" demonstration of Rousseau's passionate intuitions. Nature favors all the animals left in its care; the wild horse, cat, bull and even the donkey are stronger, more vigorous and courageous in the forests than in captivity.

When he denies the august title of "lion" to the puma, the naturalist Buffon criticizes the old confusion originating from the application of familiar European names to new species, never seen before. Names had confused matters—he affirmed—leading to erroneous descriptions by travelers and ethnologists. Though such confusion was psychologically excusable given the greater readiness with which people notice likenesses rather than differences, it was lamented as early as the late 16th century by Father José de Acosta in *Historia natural y moral de las Indias* (1590). After Buffon, this criticism was taken up again with vigor by Father Luis de Molina, and Thomas Jefferson.

In conclusion, in Buffon's theories we find a tendency, typical of the century, to interpret the organic link of the living being with nature, of the creature with the environment, as a rigid, necessary, causal relationship. In the same way, Montesquieu had fixed constant, deterministic relations among climates, institutions and customs, between the "nature of the terrain" and "political laws." Still, Montesquieu had emphasized the difficulty of establishing or maintaining free institutions in hot, relaxed climates, which render people lazy and vile; whereas Buffon attributed a certain degree of freedom in man from a causal subjection to nature, thus establishing man's prerogative; instead, as regards the other varieties of animals, he did not hesitate to "deduce" their characteristics from negative factors of the soil, humidity, or temperature.

It is certain, however, that despite the caution with which Buffon explained his theories, these somehow implied a scientific revolution, because for the first time Nature, a work of the Creator, no longer appeared totally and eternally fixed in immobile perfection.

After Buffon, the denigration of all of American nature rapidly reached an extreme, with the *Recherches philosophiques sur les Américains ou Mémoires intéressants pour servir à l'histoire de l'Espèce Humaine*, by Abbot Cornelius de Pauw, published in

Berlin in 1768. De Pauw was a typical Encyclopedist, not so much in his frequent attacks against religion and the Jesuits, or his free-handedness—even pedantry—in furnishing details on peculiar sexual habits and aberrations, but because he united the most solid kind of faith in "progress" with a complete absence of faith in the natural goodness of man. "Man in himself is nothing; he owes what he is to society: the greatest metaphysician, the greatest philosopher, abandoned for ten years on the island of Fernandez, would come back wild, mute, an imbecile." Thus the American savages are little more than beasts that hate the laws of society and the constrictions of education, each living for himself in the absence of any mutual assistance, in a state of inertia and complete wretchedness. De Pauw is thus much more radical than Buffon. The American is not even an immature animal, a child; he is degenerate. Nature in the Western Hemisphere is not imperfect, as Buffon thought, but decayed. Throughout de Pauw's works, implicitly or explicitly polemical against the tales of the missionaries and the admirers of the good savage, he obsessively repeats that nature in America is weak and corrupt, inferior because it is degenerate; the people are incurably lazy and incapable of any mental progress.

However, according to de Pauw, this did not give Europeans the right to mistreat them as they had done and continued doing. Even though their superiority was undeniable, they had taken undue advantage of it; faraway peoples could only complain of Europe; people must put a stop to organizing scientific expeditions to lands which (luckily for them) were still unknown; they must stop dreaming of new conquests. In this sense de Pauw, despite his Encyclopedist enthusiasm for progress, was still a humanitarian who hated wars and was not afraid to reveal their hypocrisy.

The cause of the primitives' degeneration was to be found in a catastrophe, a kind of flood that had occurred only in the Americas, and could only have led to those sad conditions foreshadowed for all the world by the first flood, after the fall of Adam.

With all these controversies, America and the Americans were depicted and fixed in the center of a vortex of issues involving zoological geography, ethnography, moral theology and the philosophy of history, and de Pauw touched the extreme limits of such diatribes. In gaining awareness of itself as a new civilization, its universal mission no longer confined to Christianity, the Europe of the Enlightenment realized it needed to include the overseas world in its plans, and to organize all the new knowledge it had drawn from it. Moreover, America was the daughter of Europe, while Africa and Asia clearly were not. It was Europe and at the same time, non–Europe; it could therefore be entrusted with an ideal mission, a heritage from Europe which neither Asia nor Africa had ever been qualified to receive. What basically motivated the dispute was a demand for synthesis. In order to make the world as a whole conceivable in relation to Europe, it now appeared necessary to consider each and every part of the world. What had been Bodin's aspiration now returned in a critical form as a problem to be resolved. Once the Americas had been discovered, the world was complete; all men were marvelously united, taking part in the universal Republic, as if they formed a single city.

The work which popularized Buffon's and de Pauw's ideas throughout Europe was the extremely popular *History of America* by William Robertson (1777). Easy-to-read, elegant in style, it was published at the moment of greatest interest in America (the year after the Declaration of Independence; in fact, the war that followed led Robertson to publish his work about the Spanish conquests in incomplete form). The book was immediately translated into many languages, and reprinted continuously until the middle of the 19th century. Inspired by Voltaire and completely contrary to Rousseau's concepts, Robertson emphasized the vastness of the American continent as its principal trait. Nature has left a huge footprint on everything; everything, from the mountains to rivers to lakes, has gigantic proportions. But—and this is the first reservation—what marks the American continent is its cold climate. The latitudes at which grapes and fig trees grow on other continents are covered by snow there for six months a year. The inhabitants, vulgar and indolent, do nothing to improve the land, which thus is hostile and unhealthy nearly everywhere for Europeans, and strangely weak in all its plant production. Taking up Buffon's ideas, Robertson emphasizes the fact that there are no ferocious beasts; and the beasts of European origin—bears, wolves, deer—have grown smaller or degenerate. The climatic factors themselves, which have not allowed the birth of any nobler animals, have favored the multiplication and development of reptiles and insects. And the birds, even while forming a separate category because some of them are large and extraordinarily colorful, nevertheless have the incurable defect (already stressed with stupor and anguish by numerous travelers) of not knowing how to sing. This deficiency of American birds, which had struck Buffon and had been attributed to the cold, damp climate, harmful to the sex organs of birds (aside from the bad example given by the harsh voices of the savages), was now taken to typify the sadness and muteness of all of American nature, a poetic symbol of its impotence at self-expression.

When he comes to deal with the natives. Robertson is, however, much more cautious than de Pauw. He gathers and evaluates a great deal of evidence, and rejects all those singularities, such as monsters and giants, whose existence is not sufficiently proven. Thus, he denies the existence of Patagonian giants, citing sources gathered by de Pauw, while he does accept de Pauw's concept of the American origin of syphilis—which alone would have outweighed all the "benefits" brought by America.

He prepares questionnaires on the American native. Is he robust and vigorous? Is he beardless by nature? Is he deficient in amorous passion? Together with questions regarding animals, he sends out these questionnaires to travelers, missionaries, officers in the colonies, and then collects their answers. However, despite Robertson's effort at objectivity, he has no sympathy for the object of his investigation; nor is it the ideal of progress which makes him so insensitive toward the "savage." Instead, in his work we find civilization and barbarianism in net opposition to one another; there is no gradation or passage between one and the other. Nature makes men equal, and their capacities for improvement appear to be the same everywhere; but if we take a look at the savages, we must admit that human intellectual powers find extremely limited expression in their works. Even among the Mexicans and Peruvians, there can be no comparison with the ancient world; they, too, have remained in the infancy of civilized life. The highly praised Mexican works of art are inferior to the roughest Egyptian sculptures. Furthermore, it is not worth the trouble to worry about their religious ideas, as Father Lafiteau did in *Moeurs des Sauvages Amériquains;* in the end, the native is a melancholy animal, possessing many great mental gifts, but not the fundamental one: an eagerness to achieve something useful and to improve his fate. The most outstanding trait of the American natives thus turns out to be an inherent apathy, due in part to climate, in part to the easiness of subsisting without making any great effort. They have not domesticated any animals because the savage in his true state is the enemy of other animals, not their superior. He destroys them, but does not know how to breed them or raise them. The true domestic animals of the natives are their women, whom they treat like beasts of burden, humiliating and despising them, devoid as they are of any amorous sensitivity. Apathetic even in the latter, indeed, they amazed missionaries with their frigidity. Once again, their hairlessness is stressed. They are perfectly smooth in every part of their body, an unmistakable sign of their deficient virility. They are therefore similar to children; which is, from a rationalist's point of view, a condemnation.

CHAPTER IV

The Nineteenth Century

The Birth of Linguistic Anthropology

Between the end of the 18th century and 1859, which represented, in a certain sense, a turning point between two eras in the history of anthropology, the different disciplines now making up anthropological science gained recognition. Each one grew in its own specialized area, and the first "classic" works were elaborated.

In physical anthropology, after the theories on the monogenetic or polygenetic origin of humanity, and after the opposition put up by Jean-Baptiste and Georges, a series of works and discoveries sprang up: methods for measuring cranial capacity, the invention of the compass for measuring thickness, calculation of the cephalic index, important collections of skulls, and finally, the passing fashion of phrenology. Man had come down from his pedestal now; the study of man was no longer a sacred thing—except in certain areas, such as the ethnology of sexuality which, with the brilliant exception of Bronislaw Malinowski, had just recently begun. Two other neglected areas were the juridical and economic ones. As regards these, we must keep in mind that it was not the vast systematic organizations of ideas achieved in the 19th century—which reconstructed hypothetical evolutionary sequences—that could substitute serious research on economic ethnography. The latter discipline concentrated on analyzing the circulation of possessions; with few exceptions, its origins, too, are quite recent.

A number of scholarly societies now began to form. In 1822, the British Association for the Advancement of Science created an anthropology section; in 1839 the Ethnological Society of Paris was founded. The Ethnological Society of London originated in 1843. The science of languages, of which the "Observateurs de l'Homme" had been forerunners, gained new solidity after the discovery of Sanskrit; but incredible though it may seem, scholars did not become aware of the relation between language and culture till a very late date. Language is the primary element in the life of a community; it is the fundamental instrument of interaction between people; it is impossible to imagine a social group which does not adopt at least one linguistic variety in its daily exchanges. Naturally, an entire realm of non-verbal signs exists, such as those studied by proxemics and kinesics. This realm—which Malinowski was the first to note—is very important in cultural communication and exchange; however, most of the communicative weight falls on the spoken language. It is mainly through language, in fact, that the education of children takes place; in learning the language (or languages) of their community, children gradually acquire all organizational criteria, rules for behavior, norms for acting and thinking, and the principal ideals inspiring and upholding the collectivity. Learning the words that indicate kinship, and terms of respect toward the elderly, for example, is very important because it illuminates the way in which members of the community are linked by differentiated relations, and organized into a system. Similarly, learning the concepts of "right" and "wrong" means assuming the hierarchy of values and norms of conduct associated with them. Learning a language, in other words, is one of the principal instruments for absorbing culture.

And yet despite its importance, the cultural aspect of language use has been the most seriously neglected one in linguistics and anthropology. For a long time, linguists held that their proper object of study was language as a system separate unto itself, without taking into consideration the culture which adopts it or the purposes it serves. Everything that could not be enunciated in terms of phonology, morphology and syntax was believed to be "extralinguistic," and therefore outside the competence of the linguist. Even "meaning" has been considered extralinguistic by many, because it is not analyzable with the same methods with which sentence structure is analyzed. Among the structuralists, even Leonard Bloomfield, who nonetheless grasped more than anyone else the relationship between language and culture, was mostly preoccupied with giving a scientific status to the linguistic discipline, removing it from the realm of any psychological or philosophical speculation which could not provide sufficient linguistic-structural guarantees. This approach gave rise to a strong tendency to study empirical facts only in their most directly observable aspects, and the formal relations among them.

The philosophy of language doubtlessly revealed a deeper understanding of the linguistic event with Ludwig Wittgenstein, John Austin, Willard Quine, and Max Black; but even in this case, proper relevance was not given to the social context of the speaker, so that the entire rapport between language and culture was lost. Moreover, one must admit that not even anthropologists were much interested in the study of language (although it was two anthropologists, Franz Boas and Malinowski, who founded a form of anthropological linguistics), generally being inclined to consider linguistics as a technical specialization for linguists alone. At any rate, we must not be surprised over this development in linguistic studies; for the inclusion of language in anthropological interests could not have occurred until a concept of culture as a total model had risen. This explains why it was Tylor, Boas, and Malinowski themselves who first realized the language-culture link. Finally, today we are becoming more and more aware that the framework in which we must place linguistic data must necessarily be the anthropological one; the best contributions in the ethnolinguistic field are often given by scholars with an anthropological background.

Interestingly enough, among elements inspiring ethnographic curiosity, attention toward the languages of other peoples was the last to be born—and not only in the West. If we consider that travelers in the past must have known other languages, it seems incredible that we are told so little about foreign languages or that, as in the case of Arab travelers, the languages of peoples visited are represented in a fantastic manner. As regards the Greeks, an exception to this lack of interest is Herodotus who, as a complete ethnographer, also gathered evidence of a linguistic nature concerning the countries touched on during his journeys. Herodotus himself probably had some notion of a foreign language—that of the

Scythians of Southern Russia—and certainly made use of good interpreters when communicating with other peoples. Furthermore, Herodotus gives indications regarding the linguistic situation of various countries; for example, he observes that the Indian peoples are numerous, and that they do not speak the same language. Observations on the languages of peoples visited during journeys are also given—albeit in a fragmentary manner—by Chinese travelers, and by the early Muslim travelers and geographers. Notable interest for the social aspects of language is also shown by the great Tunisian historian, Ibn Khaldun (1332–1406); and later, a good deal of information on European and Asiatic languages is found in the work of the Muslim traveler, Evliya Celebi (Constantinople, 1611–1679). The European missionaries and merchants who left accounts of their travels during the Middle Ages give very little data on the languages of the peoples visited. Several observations on the diffusion of the Tartars' tongue, Coman, are found in *Historia Mongalorum*, by the Franciscan, Giovanni da Pian del Carpine, sent among the Tartars in 1245 by Pope Innocent IV. Marco Polo, in contrast, showed great interest in the languages of the countries to which he traveled. He himself rapidly learned more than one language—including, most probably, Persian and Mongolian.

With the era of the great discoveries, of ocean voyages and the first colonies, contacts with other peoples became closer and closer. In travel writings we now find lists of words in one or more of the native languages, accompanied by a translation. These documents are highly important, for not only do they furnish evidence concerning the ancient phases of the language, but also allow us to deduce the presence of a determined people at a specific moment and place. Among the most famous travel accounts demonstrating an interest in language, we should mention the one by Antonio Pigafetta (Vicenza, 1480 ca.), while also considering that a great deal of material, especially writings by missionaries, still remains unexplored in the archives and libraries of the various religious orders.

Sassetti's notes on ancient Sanskrit as a language of science are well-known; however, it seems that he never personally knew any local languages of India. As mentioned before, other observations of linguistic interest were left by that other Italian globetrotter,

Franceso Carletti, who first introduced the word "chocolate" (*cioccolatta*) to Europe, and was among the first to speak extensively of Chinese ideograms and the Japanese alphabet. It was Matteo Ricci who was best acquainted with Chinese; he learned the language, and composed more than 20 works of mathematics, astronomy and other sciences. The custom of gathering lists of words to publish as an appendix to travel reports remained strong throughout the 17th century; though it must be considered that such lists reflect not so much a true linguistic interest, as a practical need, for they furnished phrases useful for travelers in establishing the first contacts with the various communities visited.

The earliest travel accounts thus had the merit of calling attention to foreign languages, presenting them as instruments of communication, and no longer as a hodge-podge of incomprehensible sounds. When the missionaries replaced these early explorers and their tales, living for many years—in some cases, for a lifetime—in mission lands, they necessarily learned the language of the sites, and produced a series of documents, letters, reports, and manuals which they sent to the central houses of their orders. Much of this material has remained unedited, and is awaiting study; what was printed often represented the first book ever printed in the language: in Burmese, Tamil, Georgian, etc. Even before studying a language and beginning to speak, the missionaries attempted to establish a grammar, and grammatical descriptions ended up conforming to fixed models taken from the traditional models of Greek and Latin grammar; this habit lasted up to the 19th century. The material which the missionaries thus made available was enormous, even though it could be printed only in part; and it extended to a great number of linguistic groups. The fact that it has been so sporadically exploited is due to the attitude of the philosophers, who underestimated the direct sources which they might have utilized, because of that lack of interest in the cultural aspects of language which we have already mentioned. Giambattista Vico himself, celebrated as one of the forerunners of modern linguistic science, did not have and was not worried about having any knowledge of the "primitive" languages on which his theories were based.

In the realm of theories concerning the relationship between climate and human groups, Lord John Arbuthnot, author of an *Essay Concerning the Effect of the Air on Human Bodies* (1733), held that languages, too, are subject to the influences of climate, and that the Nordic peoples have tongues rich with consonants but poor with vowels, because they avoid opening their mouths in order not to breathe in cold air; whereas for the opposite reason, the languages of hot countries are rich with vowels (his theory lived on for a number of years). The entire 18th century saw a growth of that repertoire of stereotypes regarding primitive languages, which was to survive until recent times. Primitive tongues "have no grammar," are pronounced using "indistinct" sounds, have a fluid, imprecise vocabulary, are incapable of abstraction, etc. But in the last years of the 18th century, as the ideology of travel developed, the collection of linguistic data was adequately theorized. The scientific instructions used by travelers included, among other recommendations, indications on the importance of learning the local language; the first such instructions are perhaps those prepared by the German Johann David Michaelis for the expedition to Arabia of the Dane Carsten Niebuhr (1774). Constantin-François de Volney, who, as we have seen, was extremely sensitive to the linguistic problem, on several occasions recalled the importance of achieving cultural contact directly through the local language; he himself was dedicated to learning Arabic in the course of his journey to Egypt and Syria (1782–85), and Amerindian languages during his journey to the United States (1795–98).

Wilhelm von Humboldt (1767–1835), perhaps the most profound and original scholar of the philosophy of language during his time, merits a place of honor by himself. He rigorously confronted the technical aspect of scientific research, as well as applying himself to the study of Chinese, Basque, Amerindian languages, and Javanese. Humboldt clearly perceived the sense of cultural importance inherent in a language; in fact, as he himself pointed out, he used language as a vehicle to travel through what is deepest and loftiest and most "varied" in the world. He thus inaugurated a zone of contact among linguistics, psychology, and ethnology. Linguistics research now found itself entering an authentically anthropological realm, as it collaborated with the effort to understand humanity in its most varied manifestations. However, Humboldt's thought found little resonance among his immediate successors, while linguistic science marched off in the historic-comparative direction.

An authentic science of linguistics began in Europe with the discovery of Sanskrit. The existence of a language with affinities to Greek and Latin in such faraway countries as India posed a problem of difficult solution for scholars of the late 18th century. It was an English magistrate, William Jones, who brought the question to light, founding the Asian Society of Calcutta in 1784. The ethnological implications of the discovery—that is, the kinship between Europeans and Indians—provoked a trauma in many individuals, but this kinship appeared more acceptable if one considered that it dated back to an unknown era of antiquity, after which there had been a long period of degeneration. This was the position of Rousseau's romantic followers, the same one that Friedrich von Schlegel expounded in his work *Über die Sprache und die Weisheit der Indier* (1809). In 1816 Franz Bopp published his *Über das Conjugationssystem der Sanskritsprache,* a work by which he founded a type of linguistics restricted exclusively to the field of language. He placed himself on an exclusively scientific terrain, declaring in 1833 that he intended to study the physical and mechanical laws supporting idioms.

Linguistics in its narrow sense, following Bopp's teachings, was introduced in France by his translator, Michel Bréal, one of the founders of the Société Linguistique of Paris, whose statute forbade any research into the "origins" of language and into the fabrication of an international, artificial language. This diffidence toward research into the origins and toward any practical applications sprang from the positivistic spirit that was to triumph during the last quarter of the 19th century. However, in the middle of the century speculations on the origins were anything but rare. Ernest Renan published *De l'origine du langage* (1848), in which he tried to prove that families of languages were irreducible in relation to one another. In the early 19th century the concept of an "Indo-European race" was still lacking; instead, the primacy of Indo-European languages—including Sanskrit—was constantly declared. They were held to be the most capable of expressing grammatical relationships in an organic way. In anthropology as well, the concept of "race," having appeared in Johann Friedrich Blumenbach (1752–1842), became current in scientific literature only toward the middle of the century; romantic literature speaks of "peoples" (*Volk*).

Renan distinguishes races from languages, but for him, language is strictly linked to society. In his *Histoire générale des langues sémitiques* (1855), on the contrary, he had expressed himself in a more pronouncedly racist manner:

> There is not one example of a savage people that has risen to a level of civilization. One must therefore suppose that the civilized races have not passed through a savage state, and that from the beginning, they have carried within themselves the seed of future progress. Is not their language alone a sign of nobility, and almost an early philosophy? To imagine a savage race that speaks a Semitic or Indo-European language is a contradictory pretense, which any person initiated in the laws of comparative philology and the general theory of the human spirit, will refuse to accept.

An ignorance of exotic languages was one of the reasons for such theories, besides the general scorn for "savages" which prevented anyone from bothering to correctly learn the primitive languages, which are, aside from anything else, quite complex. During the same period, Max Muller published his most important works. He distinguished language and race more clearly than Renan, and did not hesitate to declare that "any attempt to make racial and linguistic classification coincide is doomed to failure"; indeed, he went even further, distinguishing language from social development.

Still, given the commonly-accepted equivalence between language and race, the linguists' classifications were used by anthropologists as a useful criterion for ethnical groupings. The classification according to languages, in fact, offered them the most easily applicable criterion. The last attempt to give a universal anthropological classification was that of Friedrich Muller (1834–1898), who in 1876 proposed a division in 78 groups, established on the basis of criteria that varied from the anthropological to the geographic and to the linguistic. The first great division is between wooly-haired speakers and smooth-haired speakers. The former are distinguished between those with "tufted hair," that is, Hottentots and Papuasians, and those with "fleecy hair," that is, African blacks and Kaffirs; the latter include the "straight-haired"—i.e., Australian, "Hyperborean" Americans, Malaysians, Mongolians, and the "curly-haired"—Dravidians, Nubians and Mediterraneans. The Mediterraneans include Basques, Caucasians, Hamito-Semites and

Indo-Europeans. Attempts to link the races and languages were to be repeated again and again, before totally disappearing.

If on the part of linguists interest in the social aspects of languages was so limited, it cannot be claimed that the strictly anthropological field did much more. Even in the opinion of Tylor, one of the founders of modern anthropology—and one who also acknowledged the importance of language—linguistic data should be studied only in view of an historical reconstruction. Disinterest for linguistics was even more evident in other English anthropologists.

On the contrary, it was in the realm of American studies that collaboration between ethnographers and linguists was most fruitful. Such studies were set in motion mostly by Swiss and German emigrants. For example, Albert Gallatin, between the 18th and 19th centuries; Albert Gatschet in the 19th century; and above all, Franz Boas in the 19th and 20th centuries. Boas could not understand how anyone could study an Amerindian tribe without studying its language in such a way as to note all the ritual patterns, myths, legends, autobiographical accounts, and names of objects, plants, and animals.

Malinowski merits a place of honor in anthropological linguistics, although his works in this field have never been sufficiently appreciated. As an anthropologist, he took long study trips between 1914 and 1918: first among the Mailu and then, for two years, among the Trobriandese. In both cases Malinowski mastered the local language, and his practical knowledge allowed him to carry on his work directly by way of the language, without the risks connected with translations and interpreters. But above all, his proficiency permitted him to establish a comparison with the western languages that he knew (Polish, English, French, German); and he was led to consider the problem of translatability, since the concepts that he adopted in field work could not easily find adequate translation in a European language. Malinowski thus theorized the place of language in culture, fully realizing the ties between linguistic act and context: ties that make the first element incomprehensible without a knowledge of the second. In 1920 Malinowski wrote an article dedicated to the classifying particles of a language of the Trobriands, Kiriwina; and then, an essay on the meaning of primitive languages, in which he states that each community constitutes a phatic community: i.e., one based on linguistic contact among various members, in which every utterance gains its global sense from the context, "the situational context," in which it originated. In real life, observes Malinowski, every sentence uttered is always immersed in a situation; a complete translation cannot thus be given through the choice of possible equivalents in another language so much as by the explanation of all the facts contributing to form the meaning of the sentence in that specific situation.

In *Coral Gardens and Their Magic* (1935), Malinowski gathers all the material accumulated on Kiriwina, writing an introductory essay, "An Ethnographic Theory of Language." This important ethnolinguistic document stresses the concept of "presupposition"—as a datum already known to the speaker, and sometimes to the listener as well, which conditions the linguistic act—and that of the "pragmatic force" of language. Malinowski's work in the linguistic field, however, remained without followers, except what Raymond Firth's British school preserved in the theory of situational context.

But the greatest anthropological linguist was doubtlessly one of Boas's disciples, Edward Sapir. He was not only a brilliant researcher but, setting off from the typological diversity of the languages he knew, he was also a theoretician of general linguistics, and greatly ahead of his times. In 1921 Sapir published a work entitled *Language: An Introduction to the Study of Speech*, in which he expounded notions on the structure and typology of languages that were to be assimilated only much later. In Sapir's opinion, language is something more than an instrument for penetrating a culture; it is a bridge between the individual and his culture; indeed, the real world itself is not entirely "given" in an objective manner, but is to a great degree constructed on the basis of the group's linguistic habits. According to Sapir, no two languages are so similar that they can be considered representatives of the same social reality; the worlds in which different societies live are different worlds, and not simply the same world with different labels.

In Sapir (as in Ruth Benedict) the conception of language influences the conception of culture. Whereas Boas, in principle, had refused any form of approach to culture by way of analogy (i.e., analogy with biological evolution, with the functioning organism, etc.), Sapir, on the contrary, implicitly perceived the analogy between language and culture, illustrating the fact that both language and culture utilize only part of the infinite ensemble of possibilities; language, for example, utilizes only certain sounds; culture, only certain types of behavior. In other words, both language and culture are organized according to models or patterns, though many of these patterns are unconscious. In Sapir's opinion, any language, like any culture, constitutes a unique configuration. Thus it cannot be said that there are cultures or languages which are better or worse, developed to a greater or lesser degree, of greater or lesser primitiveness, for both language and culture are always suited to necessity. Grammar is nothing but the set of linguistic patterns shared by the community, in the same way that culture is nothing but the set of behavior patterns internalized and adopted by the group.

Sapir's theory regarding the influence of language on cultural behavior was to find its most outspoken advocate in Benjamin L. Whorf, who did not hesitate to declare that the language we speak entirely modifies and models our behavior. One of the anthropologists who made greatest use of structural linguistics in anthropology is, of course, Claude Lévi-Strauss, who recognizes linguistics as a guiding discipline, and discerns structural homologies between language and culture, especially in certain of its highly-organized forms, such as kinship, myth, taxonomies, etc.

At the same time, we must recognize that studies relating linguistics and anthropology remained fragmentary and discordant for a long period, marked by dispute even among those who claimed the need for anthropologists to learn beforehand the language of the culture to be studied. In the wake of Boas, Robert H. Lowie and Alfred L. Kroeber were occupied with linguistics as well; globally, aside from the school of Boas, we can say that until recent times, the importance of language as an ethnological instrument has been underestimated nearly everywhere.

Encyclopedic Collections of Klemm and Waitz

During the early 19th century several theoreticians, basing themselves on ethnographical documents collected from travelers, codified systems which came to stand among the first treatises on natural history and comparative ethnology, and which have greatly influenced all those scholars who attempted to understand human group behavior. Gustave Klemm and Theodor Waitz, in this perspective, have left us works whose interest is not merely historical. They are similar in having accumulated facts and compiled works from different sources, but they differ both on the level of elaboration of the documents thus gathered, and on the level of personal tendency. For while Klemm accumulates, Waitz interprets; furthermore, Klemm is interested mostly in material culture, while Waitz tends to discover psychological explanations for group behavior.

Gustave E. Klemm (1802–1867), an indefatigable reader, possessed an extraordinary literary culture. From the travel accounts of ethnologists and missionaries, he extracted all the notes referring to the cultural aspects of the populaces visited, classifying them minutely and with extreme precision. His work, *Allgemeine Kulturgeschichte der Menschheit* (in ten volumes, 1843–1852), is presented as an ensemble of pure compilation and theoretical thought, which attempts to frame human evolution as a general picture. Klemm expounds on that three-stage cultural sequence, which was to be taken up repeatedly after his time (hunters-fishermen, animal breeders, and farmers); he divides humanity into two types of population: active and passive. The former are seen as evolved groups, the promoters of technical innovations; while the latter are subjected races, though indispensable ones on the road to progress. Klemm then theorizes an overall division of cultural history, comprising the three stages of savagery, self-domestication, and liberty. The first stage is characterized by the existence of anarchical family hordes, with no laws and no tribal organization, who survive by raiding, gathering, or hunting. In the second stage, people subject themselves to their own laws; this is the tribal phase, a social one marked by a recognizance of coherent laws, the raising of animals, agriculture, and writing. The third stage is marked by the loss of power by priests who had dominated the society during the preceding era.

Klemm also strove to gain a deeper understanding of the notion of "culture," defining it as a set of laws from past generations that is transmitted to modern generations. This was an early way of indicating that culture sums up in the individual everything that comes to him from the group. Finally, attracted by the material aspect of civilization, Klemm gathered a considerable body of evidence, becoming a precursor of technologists. This work was highly important, even though he fell into some of the errors and prejudices of his time, which were the fruit of preceding centuries. For example, in his opinion the Andaman have no sense of shame, the Amazonian natives know neither friendship nor love, and he thinks it impossible to find a trace of religious spirit among a number of primitive peoples, including the Eskimos and Iroquois.

The opening sentence of *Allgemeine Kulturgeschichte der Menschheit* claims that the author's aim is to represent the gradual development of humanity, understood as a whole. Klemm declares that Voltaire was the first to set aside dynasties and lists of kings and battles, in order to seek out what is essential in history: i.e., "culture" as manifested in customs, beliefs, and forms of government. Doubtlessly, Klemm's affirmations notably influenced Tylor, who in his *Researches* refers to the incalculable collection of data on history and civilization contained in the German scholar's writings. Moreover, as regards the phases in the history of the culture concept, Klemm must be numbered among the beginners of the third phase—the one which, around 1850, attributed to "culture" a meaning increasingly closer to the one prevalent in anthropology today. In this respect it may be opportune to cite several examples of the way in which Klemm uses the word *Kultur*, since he assumes an intermediate position between the use made in the late 18th century by Johann Gottfried Herder, K.F. von Irwing, Christopher Meiners and others, in the sense of *Cultivation* (education), and the modern definition following Tylor. Among the hundreds of cases in which the term recurs in the first volume of his *Kulturgeschichte*, A.L. Kroeber and Clyde Kluckhohn cite several examples which are indicative of Klemm's thought (*Culture: A Critical Review*, 1963). First of all, they note that references to "stages of culture" are highly frequent. These can be interpreted as "conditions" of culture (in the sense in which we also use the term "stages"); they can also refer exclusively to successive moments of the educative process. Thus we have: a very low stage of culture, the stage of European culture, intermediate stages, more elevated stages, an early stage, our stage, a certain degree of culture, etc. Analogous expressions are found in reference to steps made toward cultural progress; or we find such forms as true culture, cultural intent, cultural measuring stick, spiritual culture, moral culture, and cultural stasis. Yet we also find passages in which "culture" is used in the modern anthropological sense; for instance: "I shall try to examine and trace the gradual development of humanity from the first rough beginnings to its organization into nationalities which are organic from every point of view—that is, in relation to customs, knowledge and capacities, to domestic and public life; in war and peace; to religion, science and art."

This listing almost coincides with the final one in Tylor's famous definition in *Primitive Culture*.

The instruments of culture, continues Klemm, originated in private life and in the family; every human culture arises from the fact that it "possesses." As regards the nations of the "passive race," Klemm observes that custom is the tyrant of culture. What Klemm then clarifies very effectively is that he intends to deal with the gradual development of humanity as if this were a single individual: "I consider humanity as an individual who experiences infancy, youth, maturity." In most of his examples, Klemm thus seems to attribute to the word "culture" its modern anthropological sense. At any rate, as Kroeber and Kluckhohn note, he probably found himself assuming an intermediate position, sometimes using the term with connotations proper to the 18th century, other times to the 19th; and perhaps, without ever being fully aware of the transformation in meaning, without ever formally defining it. In Tylor's opinion, instead, Klemm carried out ethnographic work in the "modern" sense, and adopted the word "culture" as a generic term, free of any implication of progress which, on the contrary, is linked to the English term "civilization." That is why Tylor substituted the term "culture" as used by Klemm, for the term "civilization" which he himself had adopted up till then. To "culture" he gave a formal definition, fixing the concept and using it in the very title of his book, *Primitive Culture* (1871). In Klemm's hands, then, history had begun to transform itself into comparative ethnography.

Theodore Waitz (1821–1864), unlike Klemm, is concerned most of all with the psychology of primitives, in the six volumes of his *Anthropologie des Naturvolker* (1858–1871). Waitz is fundamentally a philosopher who realized how greatly the observation of exotic societies can enrich our awareness, and help us to formulate authentic psychic laws. Waitz also had the merit of avoiding all the exaggerations which were so common in his time; even though he admits the influence of the environment, he is able to stay clear of the excessive position of his contemporaries, who often claimed they could explain any cultural trait by the condition of the geographical environment. Thus for the first time we find an explicit expression of what later would be called "possiblism," in opposition to geographical "determinism": the environment "offers," according to Waitz, but does not "impose." Furthermore, he proved the wrongness of certain absurd affirmations of the time concerning blacks, both regarding their racial ancestry and their psychic capacities. However, even though he made some reservations opposing the most extremist conclusions of racism, Waitz never doubted that there were "superior" human races and "inferior" ones, even while remaining convinced that in the beginning, the physical gifts of the various races were probably equal, or nearly so.

Waitz thus held that differences in the evolutionary process from the primitive state depended on the natural and social conditions in which peoples found themselves. Though he thought there was no proof of the fact that the so-called "inferior" races were condemned to remain in their current state, he nevertheless repeated that the development of civilization—with a few, unimportant exceptions—was limited above all to the Caucasian race.

While Klemm's work is dated 1843, Waitz's great anthropological inventory appeared from 1858 onward. The year 1859 thus seems to open a new era: the publication of Darwin's *Origin of the Species* coincided with the foundation of the "Zeitschrift fur Volkerpsychologie" in Germany, and with a whole series of ethnological events, including the creation of the Anthropology Society in Paris. In 1859 Paul Broca also traced a complete scheme for anthropological science, revealing an extraordinarily broad vision for his time—and a methodologically valid one. Indeed, Broca conceived anthropology as a science of synthesis, one giving full meaning to the partial results of the study of races, prehistory, linguistics, and ethnography. The major anthropologists were to take up this perspective.

Evolutionism and Comparativism

From the still-hesitant advent of the human sciences—which little by little began to be differentiated—until the birth of a specialized anthropology, the guiding concepts have undergone profound transformations. Throughout the second part of the 19th century, the premises of evolution unmistakably provided the dominant note, and their echo was strong enough to stifle the discordant voices that rose here and there. After the end of the 1800s, on the contrary, it was humanity's global organization in society that was reconsidered; new theories arose, tending to give a different interpretation of social facts and their interrelation. One must therefore start out by mentioning the principal authors of anthropology in the area of evolutionism, to try to trace a pattern of tendencies, indicating the direction taken by different currents of thought.

Definitions of the concept of "evolution" are numerous and sometimes contradictory. In synthesis, the history of evolutionism in anthropology can be considered as the history of attempts to determine the laws regulating mutation, and to find a scale in order to establish the directions in which they are headed; i.e., to measure "progress."

In the 1800s the concept of evolution constituted a meeting point between various scientific disciplines, and represented the nucleus around which a new world vision was beginning to form. The idea that nature—physical and biological—was subject to mutations, and that these mutations were explainable by material causes depending on the same laws operating in the present, constituted a true revolution. From Charles Lyell and Darwin onward, it became clear that even nature had its history, being subject to evolutionary processes; the history of mankind, which had been assigned a progressive character from the Enlightenment on, became nothing other than a part of natural history. As mentioned before, the evolutionary ideas elaborated during this century had many forerunners; only in this period were they expressed in systematic form and subjected to verification, rising to the rank of scientific theories.

Inorganic evolution is linked to the name of Lyell, organic evolution to Darwin, and superorganic to Herbert Spencer. Lyell's contribution was fundamental: his work directly influenced both Spencer and Darwin. Lyell, a geologist, was opposed to "catastrophism," then advanced by Georges Cuvier, according to which the present aspect of the earth results from a series of successive geological cataclysms occurring through divine intervention. Lyell, instead, held in *Principles of Geology* (1830–1833) that modifications in the earth's crust had been caused by the same processes which operate today (actualism or uniformism). Given the extreme slowness with which these causes function, it was necessary to acknowledge that the earth is extremely ancient, thus going beyond the limits (till then constantly respected) of biblical chronology, which assigned an age of 6000 years to the world. Lyell's theory thus offered that temporal depth which was indispensable for the development of the evolutionary theory in biology and anthropology, and revolutionized sciences like paleo-ethnology and prehistory. Therefore the two centuries separating Isaac Newton and Charles Darwin represent the culminating period in which a process of profound transformation was achieved in the study and vision of society and natural reality. This "scientific revolution," this transformation, consisted essentially in the passage from a static concept of the world to a dynamic one. The two centuries saw a progressive decline of static creationism, and the arduous emergence (in astronomy, geology, anthropology and biology) of the new historical conception of nature and humanity. Toward the middle of the 19th century it found its most coherent, rigorous expression in Darwin's evolutionary theory.

This period saw the emergence of stages in a long, tormented process of discovery of time and mutation, stages necessary for the formulation of the theory itself. All its elements were already present in the scientific world around 1818: Georges-Louis Buffon, Immanuel Kant, and Pierre-Simon de Laplace had derived the origin of the solar system from the action of a universal system of laws, elements, and forces; James Hutton had conceived the surface of the earth as a system of matter in motion which had existed for millions of years; Cuvier had applied the resources of comparative anatomy to the reconstruction of extinct species and, together with William Smith, had understood how to interpret fossil evidence hidden in the earth's crust. Buffon had suggested the variability of organic forms, and Lamarck had postulated their gradual evolution from monad to man. Buffon had also perceived that the extinction of species was linked to the struggle for survival among the various creatures produced by the infinite combination of nature. Pierre-Louis Maupertuis, James Cowles Prichard, and William Wells had, in turn, perceived the possibility that new types could take shape from casual variations emerging during the course of procreation, and Wells had even adopted the notion of natural selection to explain the origin of the black race. Thomas Malthus's essay on population already existed at the time; as is well-known, it inspired Darwin's conception of the mechanism of the origin of the species.

Although the elements of Darwin's theory were already present, no one up to then had been able to gather them into a meaningful synthesis. Moreover, the traditional concept of nature, though weakened by these developments, still exercised great influence over scientific thought. The Western world was not yet ready to give up the great doctrines of the Revelation and Creation which for centuries had determined Western man's position in relation to his universe, and which had given meaning and finality to science itself. Darwinian theory, on the contrary, besides giving definite scientific confirmation to the historical concept of natural reality, profoundly modified not only scientific ideas, but also a philosophical concept which had accompanied much of the West's cultural development: the teleological vision, the idea that a divine design, a pre-established plan, harmonically governs nature.

This idea, which had progressively been displaced from the physical world, tenaciously persisted in the world of organic life.

"Pendulums could oscillate with mathematical regularity, and mountains could rise and fall through the millenniums, but living beings were outside the rule of material principles or secular history. If life obeyed certain laws, they were supernatural ones, not tied to the physical laws of inorganic matter" (George Gaylord Simpson, *Evolution*, 1972).

On the contrary, according to a vision of the world as it

emerged on the basis of the *Origin of Species*, passage from the simplest to the most complex, from disorder to order, from chaos to finality, seemed to result from the mere effect of the interaction constituting the historical development of nature. Life, even thought itself, had arisen only in a certain phase of natural history, as a consequence of the evolution of matter; and the human being, far from being the privileged finality of creation, was nothing but the most elevated among those natural forces that had generated other living beings. This reality belonged to a world in which humanity was obliged and able to count on itself alone. With the abandonment of teleology, Darwin thus came to complete the long process of transformation of the concept of nature which had begun with the "scientific revolution," synthesizing the heterogeneous suggestions of Buffon, Cuvier, Lamarck, Lyell and many others in a materialistic theory of evolution founded on material causes, on the action of chance, and on a refusal of the premise that evolution is necessarily progressive in character. As has been accurately noted, "from 1859 on, no theory, whether biological or physical, would be able to avoid confronting the theory of evolution and its explanation of nature. The whole of culture would be obliged to acknowledge this new reality, and adapt to it" (B. Fantini, *L'Evoluzionismo*, 1976).

In turn Theodosius Dobzhansky declares: "It is difficult for our generation to realize how really new the idea of evolution is in its vastest sense of universal transformation pervading everything. The infinite is a concept that many find it hard to grasp; the myths of creation were thus constructed in order to demonstrate that man and the universe had had a beginning: once things had been created, people thought they would remain so forever" (*Mankind Evolving*, 1962).

It was Condorcet (1743–1794) who explicitly declared that the history of man is a development proceeding from an inferior state to a superior one. From savage primitive life, through degrees of increasing enlightenment, it rises to that of maximum perfection: there must be ten stages; and the tenth—the perfect one, according to Condorcet—had almost been reached.

On his part, Herbert Spencer linked inorganic matter, biological life and culture in a single cosmic system subject to the lone universal law of evolution. It was he who coined the term "superorganic," by which he indicated not only culture developed by man, but also certain forms of animal social life, such as the cooperation and division of work among social insects like bees and ants. He held that the superorganic evolution of man, though immensely surpassing all others in extension, complexity and importance (even to the point of making them relatively insignificant) is not, however, a substantially different phenomenon. Evolution being a single process that assumes three different forms, its laws are valid for inorganic matter, for biological forms and for culture as well.

Finally, Tylor was the first to understand the need to separate superorganic evolution from organic, forming a science of culture independent from biology. Tylor, too, held that if laws exist anywhere, they must exist everywhere; a positivistic conviction, this, shared by a number of anthropologists, including Emile Durkheim. But Tylor also thought that the laws regulating the development of human history could be sought out by using specific methods, proper to the discipline.

Evolutionary anthropologists, today surpassed and often criticized for not having managed to liberate themselves from the burden of certain prejudices, nonetheless accumulated a great body of knowledge. In order to interpret their evidence, they were able to mobilize all the resources of inductive and deductive reasoning—though in their enthusiasm they often failed to protect themselves with the necessary precautions. We are indebted to them, at any rate, for delineating all the problems with which we deal in anthropology even today. First of all, we must consider that nearly everyone took for granted the notions of evolution and progress that had been defined in precedence by philosophers and scientists. Anthropologists thus tried to establish (sometimes with an excess of confidence) sequences of a general order, valid throughout time and space. Their excesses were counterbalanced by the grandiose vision that they possessed of the human phenomenon; the evolutionary and comparative method, in fact, implied the notion of an integrated humanity to which the different ethnic groups contributed—in varying degrees, but with the aim of reaching the same civilization. Discernible cultural differences, they said, are the result of different situations on a temporal scale, and not of congenital predisposition. These evolutionists were thus actually anti-racists, because they all accepted the premise of the psychic unity of the human race.

Authors who followed a different orientation were very rare. Among them, one important point of reference is Johann Jakob Bachofen, who published his imposing work, *Das Mutterrecht*, in Stuttgart in 1861. In it he uses both ethnographic evidence and the classic data of ancient history. On the basis of evolutionary theory, he develops the themes of primitive promiscuity, the precedence of the female genealogical line, and the social revolution which, in his view, brought about the passage to the paternal line of descent. With a grand display of erudition Bachofen strives to interpret certain myths as evidence of what he considered to be the oldest evolutionary stages, also describing such signal institutions as the *couvade*. Of course, his entire, highly-debated hypothesis on primitive matriarchy is actually devoid of any historical validity.

Shortly after Bachofen, John McLennan proceeded in the same direction with *Primitive Marriage* (1865) and *Studies in Ancient History* (1876). McLennan was the first scholar to use the terms "endogamy" and "exogamy," which were later to enjoy great fortune. His interest, like that of nearly all the other evolutionists, was centered on kinship relations, and the hypothetical phases in the development of social organization.

During the same period Adolf Bastian (1826–1905), in *Der Mensch in der Geschichte* (1860), began to assume an original position, placing himself outside the tendencies of his time. He turns out to be a forerunner of the diffusionists, by trying to define a series of "geographic provinces" characterized by a specific set of cultural traits. According to his hypothesis, all societies started out from the same point, since in the beginning, humanity disposes of a certain number of "elementary ideas" which each group adopts in conformity with its specific needs, aspirations, and the ecological framework of its activity. Cultural exchanges—the influences that are exercised by one group over another—contribute to give a distinct image to different civilizations, which are also subject to psychological factors proper to each people. Bastian, however, is thinking in evolutionary terms as well when he postulates the existence of a general law of human development—though this development is diversified, branching out into many lines, and is not accumulative in a uniform manner. The "elementary ideas" are embodied in different cultural constructions susceptible to the conditions of time, place and environment which they encounter. Like

Friedrich Ratzel, Bastian had posed the problem of the origin of parallels between cultural facts, and had explained the analogy between (prevalently ergological) phenomena in separate and distant geographic areas among peoples that currently appear as bearers of different cultures, on the basis of the so-called "convergence" criterion. There being a fundamental unity of the human spirit, this latter, in similar environmental conditions, will react in different places and in different eras in the same manner, in the face of natural events and the need for ergological order. This would explain, for example, the appearance of instruments such as the hoe or scythe in approximately the same form, in various zones, and with no reciprocal influence.

Bastian's profession as shipboard physician allowed him to make long voyages during which he gathered numerous pieces of ethnographical data relative to the countries visited, from Australia to Africa, from Peru to Asia. Bastian utilized both his own observations and second-hand documents to demonstrate the theories he expounded in various works, including: *Das Bestandige in den Menschenrassen und die Spielweite ihrer Veranderlichkeit* (1868); *Die Kulturlander des alten Amerikas* (1878–1889); and *Die Heilige Sage der Polynesier, Kosmogonie und Theogonie* (1881).

The American author Lewis Morgan perhaps best expresses the essential theories of unilinear evolutionism. His ideas are founded on certain postulates which were later to be highly debated. Human groups pass through a series of phases which are comparable to each other; evolution is achieved by way of a process which is unilinear for each society and, globally speaking, the evolution of humanity is unidirectional as well; it is possible to define cultural "parallels" and to confront them, so that today's "retarded" groups can bear witness to the ancient state that "advanced" groups once knew; the same fundamental stimuli are at work everywhere within the various cultures (Morgan barely hinted at this concept, and failed to develop it). Phenomena of "survival" are comparable to other phenomena now perceptible in modern societies; finally, anthropology must come to discern cultural sequences, and to formulate laws of evolution. Morgan does not hesitate to extrapolate and bend the facts, forcing them to fit his schemes; the gravest thing is that he neglects the historical past of societies and civilizations without written documents, which in his view are also prehistoric. In the end, we must note that Morgan has a very simplistic vision of the different aspects—even essential ones—of primitive cultures, seriously underestimating the complexity of mythology and, in general, religious life.

Despite these methodological shortcomings, Morgan's work is important for having stressed the importance of kinship structures and the meaning of linguistic forms. Like most of the authors of his time, Morgan tended toward a general explanation. His division of human evolution into nine phases (savagery, barbarity, civilization, each divided into three periods), which proposes a classification founded on technology, is more useful than the old philosophical typologies, which nonetheless were also founded on a three-part division. Morgan distinguishes a state of savagery, a state of barbarity, and one of civilization, whose advent he dates back to the apparition of written documents. These periods are also divided in three stages each; for Morgan, such a classification implies a hierarchy of cultures. It is valid synchronically and not only diachronically. At any rate, one of Morgan's great merits was that he emphasized the importance of material culture, as seen in its repercussions on social organization. Morgan insists on the role that technological factors have played in history, influencing the juridical picture; and he attempts to clarify the relationship that must exist among technique, property and social organization. We can thus understand the interest Friedrich Engels showed for Morgan's thought, on which he relied while composing his essay on the origin of the family, private property, and the state. Morgan's two essential works are *Systems of Consanguinity and Affinity of the Human Family* (1871) and *Ancient Society* (1877).

Engels, in the preface to the first edition of his work in 1884, writes:

> The following chapters constitute, so to speak, the execution of a will. It was Karl Marx in person who reserved for himself the task of expounding the results of Morgan's research, connecting them to his (I may say, within certain limits, our) materialistic examination of history, thus fully demonstrating all their importance. Morgan, in fact, had rediscovered in his way in America the materialistic concept of history, discovered forty years before by Marx; and thanks to this, in comparing barbarity and civilization, he had arrived in the main points at the same results as Marx. And just as *Das Kapital* was plagiarized

in Germany for years by professional economists with the same diligence with which it was obstinately surrounded by silence, Morgan's *Ancient Society* was treated the same way in England by the advocates of "prehistoric" science. My work can offer only a pallid surrogate of what my deceased friend had the impossibility of doing. However, I have before me the critical notes to his detailed extracts of Morgan's work, which I reproduce here as well as possible [*Der Ursprung der Familie, des Privateigentums und des Staats*].

Engels's work thus remains marred by his ingenuous adhesion to the evolutionism characterizing the science of the moment; an evolutionism by which a total understanding of history has been attempted, precisely in the realm of utopian hope for an imminent palingenesis of humanity, a solution of final happiness intrinsic to Marx's thought. In fact, it is only when one is convinced that one has understood all of history, and the motivations of history; only when one is certain that one has understood not only the laws governing it, but human nature, that it is also possible and, apparently, right, to predict or prophesy the future. Marx's thought, indeed, cannot be separated from the evolutionary vision of history, which was part of the cultural context of his era and which (though devoid of any scientific basis) is nonetheless the only one that can justify its perspective in terms of action, and its certainties concerning the results of that action.

Evolutionism in 19th-century anthropology entails an extraordinary vision of the world, which also appears, in certain respects, in contradiction with the romanticism of the era, with its psychological turning inward toward the individual and the intimacy of the subject. Instead, evolutionary anthropology is characterized by the discarding, or even the total absence (as in Morgan, in Marx and in Engels when he writes on the origin of the family), of any psychological problem, or any intimate understanding of the person. Morgan cites "affections" or "sentiments" on very rare occasions (for example, à propos of the wish on the part of the *pater familias* to leave his possessions to his children). As regards religion, moreover, he claims that it entails irrational, incomprehensible things that one cannot take into consideration; not only does he fail to consider these, but he explains all of history as if they did not exist. Engels follows Morgan to the letter in this direction.

One must also note that, even though he knew Tylor's work and quoted it expressly, Morgan (like Engels) failed to understand the concept of "culture" as a global environment, an interdependent web of traits and institutions. Therefore, as regards the intrinsic bonds linking cultural elements, both Morgan and Engels note only those linking the production of the means for survival and the reproduction of men: "According to the materialistic conception, when all is said and done, the moment which determines history is the production and reproduction of immediate life. The latter, in turn, is of two types. On one hand, the production of means for survival, of what is necessary for nourishment, dress and shelter, as well as the instruments necessary for all this; on the other, the production of men themselves, the reproduction of the species."

Up to this point, then, in the opinion of Engels the problems of people are the same as the problems of animals; he skips over that passage (which had long been an arduous problem for scholars) according to which men live with social institutions to satisfy their "primary" needs. (Malinowski would later attempt to solve that problem.) Engels then continues by stating that the social institutions in which men live in a given historical era and country are conditioned by both types of production: on one hand, by the degree of development of labor; on the other, by the degree of development of the family.

It is also important to emphasize the fact that Engels, like Morgan, considers the historical period preceding the class struggle as being very long, whereas the period comprising the class struggle is seen as very brief, almost a parenthesis. In the view of Marx and Engels, it is about to end, so that the historical process of evolution by stages would entail time periods so incomparable with one another that the very idea of "stage" is thrown into crisis.

Moreover, comparativism, on whose basis the "primitive" is identified with "prehistoric" man, finds total agreement in Engels, so that the research on the Amerindians done by Morgan is taken to confirm the story of prehistoric man. Engels writes that Morgan's great merit is in having discovered and reestablished, in their main traits, the prehistoric foundations of our written history, and in having found in the family bonds of the Indians of North America the key to understanding the most important enigmas of the most ancient history of Greece, Rome, and Germany; enigmas which had been unsolvable up to then. In confirming his total trust in Morgan's work he adds: "His writings, of course, are not the work of a day. For around forty years Morgan struggled with his material until he came to master it completely. Precisely for this reason his book is also one of the few lasting works of our time." By the latter statement Engels showed that he was a poor prophet, for a few years later very little valid material remained of Morgan's work.

The complete acceptance by Engels of the evolutionary-comparative method finds further confirmation in the preface to the fourth edition of his *Origin of the Family* in 1891 (by then, Boas had already been at work for several years to dissolve the evolutionary method). Engels writes: "Further on in the course of this preface I offer a brief panorama of the development of the history of the family from Bachofen to Morgan, mainly because the British school of prehistoric studies, with its chauvinistic hue, still continues to do its best to ignore the revolution in opinions on prehistory set into motion by Morgan's discoveries; up to now, this has in no way prevented it from adopting Morgan's results as its own."

In the same preface, Engels adds:

> It is not possible to speak of a history of the family until the beginning of the Sixties. In this sector historical science was still completely under the influence of the five books of Moses ... The fact that among single populaces of ancient history, as among some savages still existing today [here we see that Engels considers the "savages" as survivors from prehistory], descent is not determined by the father, but by the mother; that therefore the female line was taken to be the only valid one; that among many peoples of our time marriage within certain larger groups is forbidden ... and that this custom is found in every part of the world—these facts were known, it is true; and more and more examples of them were gathered. But no one knew what to do with them; and even in the *Researches into the Early History of Mankind* by E.B. Tylor, such realities simply appear as "strange customs" standing beside the prohibition, observed among some savages, to touch burning wood with an iron tool, or similar religious silliness.

It is clear here that though he knew Tylor well, Engels was unable to appreciate the modernity of his method, and considered Tylor's effort to understand one of the fundamental phenomena of culture—religious behavior and tabooistic meanings—as "silliness." Therefore Engels states: "The history of the family was born in 1861 when Bachofen's *Mutterrecht* appeared."

Engels cannot share Bachofen's opinions since, as he notes, an interpretation viewing religion as the decisive lever of world history must find its final outlet in mysticism. However, he does recognize Bachofen as a precursor

> for having substituted idle talk of an unknown primitive state, dominated by licentious sexual relations, with proof that ancient classical literature presents us with an abundance of examples showing that before monogamy, there actually existed among the Greeks and Asians a state in which, not only did a man have sexual relations with several women, but a woman with several men, without violating the customs; that this custom did not disappear without leaving some trace in that limited idea of themselves with which women acquired the right to monogamy; that therefore, in the origins, descent could be determined only through the female line from mother to mother; that this exclusive validity of the female lineage lasted for a long time during the period of monogamy, paternity being assured or recognized; and that this original status of mothers as the only sure parents of children assured them, and thus women in general, a higher social position than they would ever again possess.

Engels is also interested in the theory of Sir John Lubbock (*The Origin of Civilization*, 1870), which states that marriage of a group of men to a group of women is an historical reality; and he names another source in Marc Antoine L. Giraud-Teulon, an evolutionary author who has been completely forgotten today, but was frequently quoted at the time (*Origines de la famille*, 1874). In mentioning Morgan again, Engels does not hesitate to declare that Morgan's discovery of an original, matriarchal *gens* at a stage preceding that of the *gens* of patriarchal law among civilized peoples has the same importance for prehistoric science as Darwin's theory of evolution has had for biology, and Marx's theory of surplus value for political economics. Engels, then, has no doubts concerning the work of Bachofen and Morgan; but above all, he has no doubt either concerning the historic-evolutionary method used to reconstruct primordial history, or concerning the identification of "savages" with men of prehistoric times. Therefore nothing valid remains of his work as a theoretical ethnologist, since today, all theories on the existence and priority of matriarchy, like the evolutionary method for the reconstruction of history, have fallen into oblivion, being considered devoid of any historical or scientific basis.

Henry S. Maine should be remembered among the evolutionists. He published his *Ancient Law* at a moment when the first works of Adolf Bastian and Johann Bachofen were coming out, in 1861; his two other important works were published later on: *Early History of Institutions* in 1875 and *On Early Law and Custom* in 1883. He can be considered the founder of juridical ethnology, having stressed the importance of a number of specific traits in the structures of traditional law, by studying the formation of the contract, the processes of incrimination and the importance of formalism in the ancient law codes. Moreover, Maine participated in the debate among anthropologists over the precedence of matriarchy, contesting the principal of matrilinear affiliation as a primary institution.

In a different area, that of the ancient history of races and techniques, John Lubbock (mentioned before as one of Engels' sources) proves himself to be an orthodox evolutionist with two works on prehistoric times: *Prehistoric Times as Illustrated by Ancient Remains and the Manners and Customs of Modern Savages* (1865) and *The Origin of Civilization and the Primitive Condition of Man* (1870).

Meanwhile, Germany saw the growth of a current of thought which, though working within evolutionary frameworks, contained the seed of diffusionism. Friedrich Ratzel published his *Anthropogeographie* in 1899. His efforts were centered on concrete research: the analysis of relations existing between the group and its environment. Much earlier, Bodin and Montesquieu had thought they could explain the history of Greece through its geography. The sterility of the soil in Attica, they thought, established a popular government there; the fertility of Sparta's soil, an aristocratic government. Hippolyte Taine stopped to consider these claims as well, but Hegel cut them short by observing: "don't come to tell me about the sky of Greece, because it's the Turks who now live where the Greeks once lived. Let them not say another word about the matter, and leave us alone!" However, in the period from 1882 to 1891, Ratzel put forward a rather simple type of determinism, a kind of fatalism that could be summed up in the formula: "the environment makes man." Ratzel cannot be classified either as an evolutionist or as a diffusionist; but he should be remembered both as a comparativist and because his thought profoundly influenced anthropologists of the succeeding generation.

Alfred Vierkandt, in turn, went beyond the current three-part classification by preparing a dualistic division of societies, founded on technological criteria; he distinguished the *Naturvolker* from the *Kulturvolker*. These terms appear in the title of his work published in Berlin in 1898. A disciple of Ratzel's, Heinrich Schurtz, turned instead to the study of social morphology, analyzing classes and castes in the archaic world (*Altersklassen und Manneerbunde*, 1902). During the same period we find works of different tendencies: that of Albert Post, dedicated to juridical organization (*Afrikanische Jurisprudenz*, 1887; *Grundriss der Ethnologischen Jurisprudenz*, 1891–1895), and that of Richard Thurnwald, dealing both with a techno-economic picture of society and with political structures. At any rate, these authors go outside the bounds of a strictly evolutionary perspective. Thurnwald, in fact, can be considered in some ways as a precursor of psychological functionalism (*Psychologie des Primitiven Menschen*, 1922; *Economics in Primitive Communities*, 1932).

Still, it is in Tylor's work (written during the same period as the vast syntheses of Bastian, Bachofen, McLennan and Morgan) that we note a new orientation, unchained from unilinear premises; it would soon take precedence. In his two great works, *Researches into the Early History of Mankind and the Development of Civilization* (1865) and *Primitive Culture* (1871), Tylor appears as an enlightened, unprejudiced evolutionist who understands the importance of the phenomena of cultural diffusion. He augurs the advent of applied anthropology; he strives to give an interpretation of religious facts; he studies kinship relations, proposing a new terminology (the word "technonimia" is his, as are the expressions "parallel cousins" and "crossed cousins"); finally, he was the first to try mapping out the distribution of institutions, such as the *couvade*.

CHAPTER V

The Classics of Anthropology

Franz Boas

Born in Minden, Germany, in 1858, Franz Boas received his degree with a thesis in the area of physics, on the color of seawater. But it was geography—also touched on in the study—that influenced his future career. The object of his interest was above all human or cultural geography, which logically led him to anthropology. For reasons of study he traveled to the Arctic regions, and was fascinated by Eskimo culture, so different from cultures he had known until then, and yet so well-adapted to the harsh environment from which it fulfilled its needs. From this first observation arose the problem which Boas tried to answer all his life: how to explain the cultural analogies and differences among ethnic groups which are different in physical type and natural habitat.

From his background in natural sciences Boas drew an inductive conception of science, often opposed by the importance given in the 19th century to the deductive conception of those historians and anthropologists who were the great "hypothesis builders." An important element in Boas's criticism of the 19th-century evolutionists was that they had been "chamber ethnologists." Boas and his students particularly criticized the indiscriminate utilization of second-hand evidence collected from the hands of missionaries and explorers. They, instead, defined their task as that of verifying all such sources through the direct observation of living societies and cultures in the field, on site. Boas's order "everyone to the field!"

was also inspired by his desire—or better, his eagerness—to study oral cultures before they were totally destroyed, or at least profoundly modified by the impact with Western civilization.

In his "Ethnology and Ethnography of Franz Boas," in 1963 Leslie White directed severe criticism at the research methods that have dominated American ethnology for at least 40 years. But though some of White's criticism may be justified, it is absolutely absurd to follow him when he claims that Boas's work has been totally negative and paralyzing. The work done by Boas was seminal, both in its concrete results and in its theoretical aspects which, even when serving ostensibly to eliminate prejudices and erroneous premises—in research on the races, for instance—have defined once and for all, the areas proper to anthropological inquiry.

The main elements of Boas's viewpoints in relation to 19th-century anthropology can be summed up as follows: 1) a method of research by induction, rather than deduction; i.e., theories and laws can be deduced only after gathering and analyzing the set of data provided by in-field research. This approach is entirely different from the deductive method that utilized and integrated data not gathered directly by ethnological investigation, but originating, instead, from vast cultural inventories which were composed in comparative form; 2) an effort to concretely observe and describe living cultures, according to the classification model of natural science; and refusal of the evolutionist theory according to which modern-day primitive cultures can give valid indications concerning societies of the past; and 3) a "diffusionist" method of research: If two societies which were geographically separated had certain cultural traits or social institutions in common, Boas's disciples sought out the common nucleus of their origin, from which they had supposedly spread out. Only when the geographical distance seemed too great to allow a hypothesis of diffusion could any "autonomous invention" be admitted.

As a consequence of the primacy given to field work, scholars came to unite physical and cultural anthropology, archeology, linguistics, and other sciences, thus establishing solid basis for modern anthropology, considered as a holistic discipline. Boas's contributions thus remain fundamental in nearly all areas of anthropology, partly because of his enormous capacity for work, and the obstinate, meticulous scholarly will which always kept him from over-relying on the data he had gathered before he had been able to analyze it. In this respect, the work done by Boas in linguistics is enlightening.

As early as 1889, Boas had written an essay dedicated to destroying the recurrent myth of the fluidity of sounds in primitive languages, demonstrating that this so-called fluidity was only an acoustic illusion. Much of Boas's activity was then dedicated to gathering information on Amerindian languages (original texts, grammatical diagrams, and ancient evidence). With painful anxiety, Boas realized that the Amerindian languages were condemned to rapid extinction; indeed, many of the texts he collected represent today the last monument to extinct languages (Kathlamet, of which he collected texts in 1890 to 1894, was even then spoken by only three people). His plan of salvation for the Amerindian languages contemplated a vast collection of grammars entitled *Handbook of American Indian Languages*, of which only three entire volumes and part of a fourth were published. Boas's approximately 80-page introduction to the first volume, in 1911, is a classical text of anthropological linguistics. Alongside technical indications on how to transcribe in a uniform manner the sounds of various languages, Boas takes up a position on a great number of problems: the relation between language and race; grammatical categories; classification of languages; influences between languages; influences of the environment on language; relationship between linguistics and ethnology, between language and thought, and so on. Another important text is the section dedicated to language in *General Anthropology*, 1938, in which Boas clearly shows that grammatical categories oblige the speaker to make given choices.

In his investigations, Boas always set out from original texts that he collected and translated; he would never have admitted any doubt over whether it was necessary for the anthropologist to know the language of the society studied, since he considered such knowledge an indispensable premise. He thus arrived at the conclusion that nothing in the relationship between language and culture should be lost. In this respect, his monography on the geographical terms of the Kwakiutl (1934) is emblematic; in it, the collection of native place names becomes an instrument for the construction of the entire Kwakiutl world—real and mythical—and its vision of space. As was logical, given all the work that he had done to destroy the prejudice surrounding the relation between race and culture, he refused the classification of languages as a means for classifying races: linguistic studies, studies in physical anthropology, and studies on cultural anthropology were, from his point of view, three different instruments, all equally necessary, but which could not be used interchangeably to clarify events in the most ancient human history because their objects of inquiry were categories of different facts.

As regards "diffusion," Boas held that every culture represents an original historical development, which occurred according to the way in which the culture utilized the material made available to it, both from the outside and by its own creative abilities. Neither the notion of socio-cultural totality nor that of "pattern" were lacking in this conception. They remained in the shade, however, whereas Boas's school gave prevalence to the modifications or changes in each cultural phenomenon. At the same time, Boas pointed out that "extraneous elements are remodeled according to the pattern of the culture receiving them, under the action of forces within it": an idea which, formulated explicitly for the first time by Boas, later gave rise to important developments.

Boas was also the first person to describe the potlatch, which he had studied among the Indians of British Columbia. Later, the potlatch was discovered and described in many other regions: in Polynesia, South America, among the Berbers and even in Europe.

But doubtlessly, Boas's importance can be evaluated above all in a discussion of anthropological method and theory. According to Margaret Mead, there never was a Boasian method or school; and on his part, A.L. Kroeber, Boas's most illustrious student, has always declared that a Boasian school was never created. But these statements lead us to believe that the particular nature of the method used by Boas—who nonetheless included among his students all the most important anthropologists of the first half of the 20th century—lay precisely in the fact that under his influence, no methodological choice was agreed on a priori. For Boas believed that the most important thing to do was to gather data effectively. The image of Boas that his students most appreciated was that of the professional scientist, who had raised the methods of anthropological research and ethnological documentation to a level at which even a physicist would have felt at ease. Actually, as we have seen, Boas's early studies were oriented toward natural science; in addition to his thesis on the color of seawater, Boas had studied physics and geography in Heidelberg and Bonn, and was also learned in mathematics. This knowledge was exploited effectively in his studies on race, and is particularly manifest in *The Mind of Primitive Man* (1911). According to Kroeber, this cultural basis provides the key to understanding Boas's role. From physics, Boas brought to anthropology a sense of precision of problems, of exact rigor of method, and a strongly critical objectivity. These qualities have always remained intact; having transmitted them to anthropology remains his fundamental, indestructible contribution to our discipline ("History and Science in Anthropology," 1935).

What was particular to Boas—notes Marvin Harris (*The Rise of Anthropological Theory: A History of Theories of Culture*, 1969)—was not the importance that he attributed to field research and data-gathering, but his insistence on the fact that this activity was more critical, more prestige-worthy and more scientific than ideating a theory at any level, whether high or low. Indeed, in the panegyric he made of the physiologist Rudolf Virchow, Boas affirms that the great progress of science obliges us to keep in mind at every moment which elements in the system of science are hypothetical and which are limited to that knowledge which is obtained by careful observation. Many impetuous students, writes Boas, have perceived Virchow's cautious, quiet criticism as an obstacle to progress. In this regard he has undergone many hostile attacks, at least until progress achieved by research demonstrated that the cautious teacher was right when he refused an important conclusion based on imperfect evidence. There are few scholars who possess that cool enthusiasm for truth which permits them to be constantly aware of the difference between an attractive theory and the observation assured by hard, honest work ("Rudolf Virchow's Anthropological Work," 1902).

In his argument against the great evolutionary hypotheses, in "The Limitations of the Comparative Method" (1896), he faced the problem of separation between examples of convergent evolution and examples of parallel evolution. Boas had no doubt that many extraordinary similarities exist between cultural traits in different cultures: similarities that could not be explained by diffusion. But the fact that certain phenomena such as shamanism, the concept of a future life, the use of the bow, geometric drawings, masks, and many other elements are vastly distributed everywhere is not sufficient to establish, once and for all, the uniformity of history. Any attempt to know whether evolutionary uniformities—that is, parallel sequences of evolution—have existed or not, must be suspended, in Boas's opinion, until data of a certain type have been collected.

The fact that many fundamental characteristics of culture are universal, he wrote, or at least recur in many isolated places, if interpreted with the assumption that the same characteristics must have always originated from the same causes, leads to the conclusion that there is a superior system according to which humanity has developed everywhere, and that all recurrent variations are nothing but minor details of this vast, uniform evolution. It is clear, continues Boas, that this theory has as its logical basis the assumption that the same phenomena are always due to the same causes.

But, says Boas, this thesis is clearly false in a great number of concrete examples. Masks, for example, are sometimes used as a disguise so that evil spirits will not recognize the person wearing one; in other cultures, instead, they are utilized to frighten people or spirits; in others again, they are worn to commemorate a dead relative. It seems quite improbable, then, that the same causal sequence could everywhere explain the development of these phenomena. It would actually be necessary to provide proof that the same phenomena have always had the same origin. But until scholars are able to do this, it is always best to suppose that historical development has gone off in various directions.

Boas's interest in mythology and folklore was based on the conviction that they would be useful in distinguishing the elements that a culture had "invented," independently of those it had received through the process of diffusion. The single elements of a myth, for example, can be found in a countless number of myths, legends and tales, but we have a mythical tale only when the various themes are associated in a given order, and this order is immutable. Boas recognizes that in its movements from one site to another, a myth can lose or gain some of its elements; but it can be said that we are dealing with the same myth each time a certain sequence of basic elements remains fixed, despite these losses and enrichments. Thus Boas's thought already contains a formulation of "structure," in which an element may favor or in some manner attract the succeeding element, but not always, and not necessarily; the fundamental principle is that of the independence of elements, in which the "structure" is conceived as an arrangement of parts forming a whole, contrary to the modern Gestalt definition in which "a whole is formed of inextricably united elements." What Boas is thinking of is actually a simple combination of elements: an ordered but contingent association of themes. Despite his continual opposition to the hypotheses of evolutionary uniformity, Boas nonetheless made no dogma out of antievolutionism.

His main interest was to achieve a high level of scientific knowledge; he insisted on declaring that if we want to achieve any progress along the line chosen, we must insist on critical methods, based not on generalities, but on each individual case. In many cases the decision will be in favor of an independent origin; in others, in favor of diffusion ("The Limitations of the Comparative Method of Anthropology," 1896).

Boas always tried to keep a balance within this intermediate position, so that, when commenting upon the work of Fritz Graebner, the principal German advocate of diffusionism, he stated that independent evolution, parallel evolution, and convergence can all be considered as normal, common cultural phenomena. At any rate, Boas liked to repeat the warning that when examining similar phenomena, it is better to exaggerate in caution, before admitting transmission as the cause for analogies.

Boas's main work thus remains in the realm of data-gathering, criticized as being so devoid of interpretative hypotheses that it dismays the reader who wishes to draw any conclusion. However, the field in which we most strongly perceive the void which Boas leaves to reconstruction is the historical one; it was precisely his different position regarding the use of history that separated Boas from his most important and famous student, Alfred Louis Kroeber.

Alfred L. Kroeber

Before Kroeber was influenced by Boas to take up anthropology, his studies were prevalently centered on the linguistic, literary, and historical areas, and this background later contributed highly to the way in which Kroeber conceived and developed the problems of anthropology. Deeply sensitive to the esthetic aspects of culture, Kroeber investigated "styles" in works on such topics as decorative symbolism among the Arapaho, changes in fashion, and the configurations of cultural development. Given this early position, it was only logical that Kroeber should tend above all to consider "history" in his attempt to understand cultures; it was precisely in his way of conceiving the place of history in anthropology that Kroeber distanced himself from Boas. Not that it was Boas's intention (as he noted repeatedly) to abandon the search for regularity in history. Boas did not propose to substitute the comparative method, but hoped that historical comparativism would complete it, thus facilitating the discovery of general laws. This, indeed, was the main objective of anthropological research. In other words, the historical method was put at the service of the comparative method. In such a way, in Boas's opinion, anthropological theory would come out of its infancy and be established on a more solid basis for generalization. However, as Kroeber well realized, Boas's way of interpreting history started out from a methodologically erroneous assumption: that he could collect data without any initial hypothesis. In this way he revealed the negative side of his background in natural science. In the end, a descriptive collection, even devoid of any classification system, could in no way be "reordered." We thus find here a misinterpretation of the scientific method which, by not allowing him to formulate generalizations (indeed, this was *not* his goal), did not allow him to "understand" the individual either. In other words, as Kroeber points out, Boas's interest in science was a symptom, if not a cause, of his incapacity to activate a deeply analytic kind of study. "When he insisted on the fact that the context could not be violated, it might seem—and perhaps he was convinced—that he was following the historical method. But this was simply an historical method assumed as a critical safeguard; the problems he addressed were not historical, except in minor cases, but rather regarded the process as such" ("History and Science in Anthropology," 1935).

The concept of "process," as constantly invoked by Kroeber, underlies the discussion over how to define the historical method in anthropology, and inevitably arises from the concept of culture.

"Culture" implies solidarity among traits, inseparable synchronicity and functionality among its diverse aspects, inextricable interaction of the parts with each other, and finally, a unitary search for "meaning" that somehow excludes the chronological connection as causality. Kroeber himself, whom this very path would lead to formulate culture as superorganic, implicitly ends up by saying as much—though in different words—when he criticizes Boas's research on primitive art. According to Kroeber, at no moment is Boas preoccupied with artistic style unless this can serve him as a point of departure for certain problems connected to the processes of conventionalization, of symbolism. Boas shows no interest for styles as such, or for their "essential quality." Kroeber's position is further clarified when he acknowledges that Boas performed the work of an historian in his monography on the Eskimos; a monography which, in Kroeber's opinion, is historical in spirit because of its coherence and lucidity, even though it deals with all problems in a synchronic perspective. Boas was disconcerted by this judgment of Kroeber's, since he could not understand why Kroeber did not assign equal historical validity to his immense work on the peoples of the Pacific Northwest.

Kroeber had unintentionally touched on what we might call the "mystery" of truly historical works: the attempt to comprehend, to give meaning to what is narrated, as Boas had done almost instinctively in his research on the Eskimos.

Actually, the exact dimension of the historical problem escaped both Boas and Kroeber, because the very concept of culture, the widening of interest in the collective products of human behavior—language, art, religion, and survival techniques—implied the need for a "descriptive" task which was quite different from the traditional one of the historian, and at the same time evaded the method of natural science, as understood in the strict meaning of the ordered classification of phenomena, and the search for regularity. Finally, the problem of the chronological succession of events, doubtlessly difficult to examine as regards the totality of a culture, was somehow underestimated in its possibility for causal explanation. This situation led Boas, for example, in his famous research on the Kwakiutl, to overlook the importance of reconstructing the "history" of Kwakiutl culture—the importance of setting out from an era remote in time from that which he considered in his field research.

At a certain point, however, Boas's wish to remain strictly tied to ethnographic facts, and the misunderstandings which he found himself facing, led him to pose the problem of *meaning*: not in "historical" terms but in psychological ones. He thus insisted for the rest of his life that the ethnologist should study the "given" as experienced by the native; and he ended up by examining the relation between psychology and culture. From this interest arose the school of "personality-culture." That is how the criterion for establishing the validity of an ethnographic work was whether or not it faithfully mirrored the natives' world *just as the natives saw it*—which meant claiming that two cultural elements are not equal if they have a *different meaning* for the ethnic groups to which they belong. In one of his last works, Boas vigorously claimed the necessity of interpreting native behavior by recurring to the categories of the native himself. In the natural sciences, he points out, we are used to demanding a classification of phenomena expressed in terminology which is concise and devoid of ambiguity. We would like there to be the same situation in anthropology. Until we cross the bounds of a culture we can classify its elements according to a clear, well-defined terminology. We know what we intend to express with such words as family, state, and government. As soon as we cross the bounds of a given culture we do not know to what extent these words may correspond to equivalent concepts. If we decide to apply our classification to extraneous cultures, adds Boas, we may end up by assimilating non-assimilatable forms ("Recent Anthropology," 1943).

For Boas the problem can be solved not by "objective" research on social structures, but on these structures' "psychological" meaning—the one experienced by men of a given cultural context. The problem of a psychological understanding of history was quite clear to Boas, and it led him, together with his most famous students, toward an excessive preoccupation with the relationship between the individual and his culture—the individual psychological reaction to the pressure of collective cultural traits. Moreover, it led him to emphasize one of the oldest questions for historians: What is the best way to reach historical "reality"—to concentrate on the subjects' life experiences, or on the narrator-interpreter's "objectivity"? The former position was chosen by Boas's famous women students: Ruth Benedict, Margaret Mead, and Ruth Bunzel. Along the path they followed toward a psychological understanding of culture, they ended up finding themselves face to face with psychoanalysis. The second position, instead, was that of another great student of Boas: Kroeber's choice of a "comprehensive" analysis of styles and cultural "configurations" presupposes an "objectification" of cultures allowing the anthropologist to find their "essence," interpret their formation and growth processes, and reconstruct their *climax*—the moment of maximum maturation and harmony.

Born in Hoboken, New Jersey, in 1876, Alfred Louis Kroeber met Franz Boas in 1896 at Columbia University, and became his student.

In his first years of activity he dedicated himself to studying the language and culture of the California Indians; but later—for approximately 30 years—Kroeber's field work expanded from the ethnographic and linguistic study of the California and Great Plains Indians to archeological research in Mexico and, above all, Peru. The publication of his monumental *Handbook of the Indians of California* in 1925 distinguished him as one of the major authorities on California ethnography.

His activities as a research scholar proceeded intensely even during his old age, till he died in Paris, after returning from a lecture, in 1960.

The theoretical interest of Kroeber's work perhaps occupies a more important place than observation and empirical analysis. This was partly because once the battle against evolutionism had terminated with Boas, it clearly became necessary to recompose and confront again the founding structure of anthropology's theoretical and methodological problems. The first edition of *Anthropology*, a vast introductory text to the discipline, dates back to 1923; the second edition, revised and updated to 1948, remains one of the most important works in the science even today.

In 1939 Kroeber published *Cultural and Natural Areas of Native North America*, in which classification according to cultural areas assumes the role not only of operative instrument, but also of theoretical theme, especially as regards the relation between cultural and natural areas, and their historical dimensions. However, the work in which Kroeber's theoretical and methodological framework appears clearest is probably *Configurations of Culture Growth*

(1944). Not only does he express here with absolute firmness the old theory of the "superorganic," which he had already proposed in 1917, but also uses in a mature manner all the conceptual instruments elaborated during his long activity—from the notion of cultural and temporal areas to that of *climax*, development, and pattern. Furthermore, all the themes for which Kroeber had waged battle, such as styles and values are treated as the prevalent themes of anthropological research.

Kroeber's work is vital above all in its treatment of the relation between anthropology and history. All of his research continually touches on the problem—until then constantly put off and left unsolved—of how to "write history." Throughout most of his life, Kroeber thus clearly saw that what separated him from Boas was the dichotomy between science and history. For that reason he was continually obliged to reconsider the concept of culture, raising it to the superorganic level (together with Kluckhohn, he systematically collected all meanings of the term "culture"). In discerning culture—in the superorganic sense—as anthropology's object of inquiry, Kroeber tried to save anthropology as a science, at the same time remaining attached to the "intuitive," "comprehensive" method of historical interpretation. The relationship between psychology and culture was divided into two sharply distinct moments: no more the objective relationship of the single individual to his culture (as is hypothesized, instead, by students of Boas with the theory of personality-culture), but problems of "psychological" understanding on the part of the anthropologist, who can perceive the "climax" or the "styles" of culture only by intuitions.

Moreover, the problem of causality also reveals to what extent Kroeber's position is one of personal analysis. In his dispute regarding the kinship terms proposed by Morgan, Kroeber continues to avoid taking a position on the problem of the cause of parallelism between social institutions and sets of terminology. It is probable, he said, that institutions mold terminology according to a causal link; but they do so first of all by influencing or allowing a *logical scheme*. In a sense, this *logical scheme* is at the base both of the institution and the terminology, so that the correlation between one and the other, though real, can be considered indirect (*The Nature of Culture*, 1952).

This approach, based on a "logical scheme" common to social structure and terminology, reflects—or rather, anticipates—the problem of "implication" of cultural traits, leaving in the background that of "causality." It always led Kroeber to dedicate attention to cultural "constants" as units of description of a culture rather than as instruments for seeking the causes of a culture.

In general, as he notes in *The Nature of Culture*, the causality present in culture has accumulated over such a long period and in such a complex way that one can actually extricate in an authentic, specific manner only a tiny part of it. Boas was great enough to realize the fact; but pioneers such as Lewis Henry Morgan, laboratory scholars such as William H. Rivers, and the mass of those cultivating the social sciences who somehow hoped to imitate the physicists have not succeeded in doing anything but produce fragments; or else their constructions are almost completely outside reality. Kroeber continues: the significant result which, globally speaking, can be obtained in the study of culture, is the pattern, not the exact causal link, as the study of linguistics should have taught us long ago.

The fact that Kroeber had clearly perceived that all the problems of anthropology were also problems of history—seen in the light of that essential factor, the concept of culture, which thus became a kind of *experimentum crucis* of history—was demonstrated by the article he wrote in 1915, "The Eighteen Professions," a kind of decalogue for anthropologists. Many of Kroeber's statements, in fact, encompass the still-unsolved points of anthropological method and theory. Thus, for instance, when he states that the purpose of history is to know the relation between social facts and the entire civilization, he is careful to point out that "relation" means real connection, not cause. What Kroeber calls "real connection" here is actually the "implication," which may be synchronic or diachronic. The same questioning approach is found in his insistence on the superorganic. History's object of inquiry is not man, but his works: that is, the result of man's actions; and even though it is the work of man and exists through man, civilization is a separate entity, belonging to a different order from that of life. History is not preoccupied with the organisms that produce civilization, but with civilization as such. The causes are the competence of the psychologist. The historian must admit a determined mental constitution, continues Kroeber, but he cannot use it as an explanation of social phenomena. At the base and at the origin of social phenomena are found true and proper instincts, which nonetheless cannot be taken into consideration or described by history.

Clearly, Kroeber refutes not the existence of instincts, but the causal investigation of cultural forces in the instincts.

From these statements we can deduce that the decisive problem for Kroeber was the concept of culture—an object of anthropological study, as it was of historical study—in which the individual disappeared as a single entity, or else was taken only as an example, but never as a cause. The problem regarding the influence of single personalities was a strictly historical one, but Kroeber confronted it explicitly, in the ambit of anthropology, because the concept of "culture" unmistakably and unavoidably brought to light a number of problems which historians had always encountered without, however, clearly realizing that they were at the base of a real epistemology of history. For example, even while admitting the superiority of the mental faculties of certain individuals, Kroeber believes that the content of inventions and discoveries does not at all derive from the minds of their supposed authors, but is "an exclusive product of the civilization" in which they live. The fact that inventions and discoveries have often been achieved in a parallel manner by different individuals demonstrates that those individuals are not at all exceptional or irreplaceable. It was precisely the examination of different parallel cases of inventions and discoveries that induced Kroeber to claim that there is a certain inexorability that prevails in the advancement of civilization. With these statements he highlighted the fact that the notion of the "superorganic" implied not only the autonomy of socio-cultural phenomena with respect to the biological world, but also the irrelevance of individuals from the point of view of cultural formation.

Moreover, Kroeber continually insists on the fact that the phenomena of culture, even though distinct from organic ones, nonetheless are part of the world of "nature." Not even the study of values, which is a central task for the anthropologist, lies outside the area of nature study. Cultural values, just like the forms and content of culture, doubtlessly exist only through the work of men and in men. As products of the human body and mind, as well as of their way of functioning, and as a specialized extension, cultural values constitute a wholly "natural" part of nature (*The Nature of Culture*).

This is possible because different levels of phenomena exist in nature; the levels (such as inorganic, organic, psychic, and superpsychic) do not represent entities which are ontologically defined and autonomous, but constitute methodological instruments for grouping together phenomena according to their traits. For this reason, says Kroeber, what is specifically characteristic of phenomena of a certain level is intelligible only in terms of other phenomena, qualities, or regularities of the same level; in denying any principle of ontological autonomy, Kroeber states that the laws of the lower levels remain valid, since they constitute the framework in which phenomena on a superior level act. Society and culture are not, therefore, independent realms in which the laws of the other sectors of nature do not intervene; on the contrary, they are nothing other than different modes of organization of matter and energy. They have their own laws or regularities, on the basis of which corresponding phenomena are determined; however, these laws do not cancel out the laws of preceding levels, but are added to them. The principle of scientific autonomy which presides over the distinction of levels, encompasses every phenomenon—or rather, every level of phenomena—within the general ambit of nature.

The distinction between organic and superorganic, contrary to the claims of many of Kroeber's critics, does not lead to any distinction between nature and culture as a distinction between spirit and nature, or between body and soul. Culture, on the contrary, is conceived as an emerging order or level of "natural phenomena"; therefore, even though culture belongs exclusively to humanity, it also continues to pertain to the natural world. For Kroeber, anthropology consequently takes shape as a "natural science," not *although* but *because* it involves humanity's non-biological or extra-somatic dimension.

Robert Lowie

Robert H. Lowie (1883–1957), like nearly all the important anthropologists of the time, was also a student of Boas, and in many of his ideas on such topics as primitive religion, on secret societies, and on totemism, he followed Boas's direction in rejecting any type of evolutionism, stressing the need to investigate the various ethnographic phenomena in their historical context. In fact, by 1917 Lowie had already found himself—simultaneously with Kroeber—defending the idea that the object of enquiry in ethnology and cultural anthropology constitutes "an independent aspect of reality" whose study requires a distinct, autonomous science. Lowie, however, remained well known above all as an ethnographer for his monography *The Crow Indians* (1935), his studies on the Indian tribes of South America, and his classic *Primitive Society*, published in 1920, in which he attempted to invalidate the theories proposed by Morgan in *Ancient Society*. Lowie's best contributions include his classification of kinship terms, which made possible later works on the relations between kinship terminology and social structure, and the innovative spirit and clarity with which he explained the roles of those groups in primitive societies which are not based on kinship. Among his most strongly contested ideas, instead—aside from his view on the role of the economy—is his hypothesis on the process of formation of the State, with which he virtually presents social stratification as a kind of cultural universal. Lowie took up these ideas on political organization later on, delving into them at a deeper level, in his *Origin of the State* (1927). Although they were highly criticized, Lowie's ideas on the State gave an orientation to specialists of primitive law and political organization, such as Edward A. Hoebel, who in his work, *Man in the Primitive World* (1949), developed the idea that the political organization is an intrinsic element of society.

Lowie is also well-known for his work in the field of primitive religion, and for having made in *The History of Ethnological Theory* (1937) an early, lively attempt to trace a history of anthropology. Later, it was widely utilized by many.

As pointed out earlier, in *Primitive Society* Lowie examines and criticizes Morgan's theses on the way in which institutions supposedly succeeded one other in the development of culture; he proposes a different sequence for this succession. He refutes the concept—shared not only by Morgan, but also, as we have seen, by many other 19th-century theoreticians such as Lubbock and McLennan—according to which the most ancient form of matrimony was group promiscuity. Furthermore, he refutes Morgan's thesis regarding a successive stage of group marriage with the participation of brothers and sisters, basing his argument on the fact that Morgan's interpretation of the so-called Hawaiian or Malaysian kinship terms is not sustainable. Since among nearly all the primitives, we find the presence of some form of nuclear family, Lowie arrives at the conclusion that the family is a primordial human group. In confronting the old, often-discussed problem of the priority of matrilinear descent over patrilinear, he accurately examines the thesis proposed by Eduard Hahn (*Das Alter der wirtschaftlichen Kultur der Menschheit*, 1905), according to which plow-based agriculture, surely of more recent origin, is often linked to patrilinear descent, while hoe-based cultivation, a more primordial kind of labor done by women, is associated with descent through the maternal line; yet he comes to the conclusion that there are too many exceptions to allow giving universal value to this sequence.

Lowie always fought against any ethnographic explanation founded exclusively on economic determinism. He was convinced above all that, in the elaboration of primitive hierarchical systems, the thirst for "prestige" was strong enough to cast a shadow onto the utilitarian aspects of stratification and division according to rank. Furthermore, he was convinced that even primitive war was in many respects a kind of sport inspired by prestige, and held that magic-religious and ideological factors kept many cultures from administering their productive resources in conformity to objectively utilitarian criteria. In *Primitive Society*, for example, he does not hesitate to claim that the potlatch as an institution had nothing to do with the economy, since it found justification in psychological motives of prestige. However, despite his polemical position in the face of economic determinism, in his last important publication, *Social Organization* (1948), Lowie appears more attentive to economic factors and, as he himself declares in the preface, he is led to take them into account not in the abstract (which was quite obvious), but by hypothesizing that given transformations of economic life have led to specific modifications in social life, going so far as to influence the expression of affection.

In addition, Lowie's studies on early religious forms are highly important, especially as expounded in *Primitive Religion* (1924). In the introduction, referring to a highly-debated question of the moment, he writes that it is very difficult to explain what the word "religion" means. A formal definition of religion would be inconsistent in principle, he writes, just as a corresponding definition of conscience would be in a psychology text, or electricity in a physics text. The rich content of these comprehensive concepts can be appreciated only after having reached a global vision of the relevant data.

At the end of his inquiry, even when he has examined several concrete cultural examples, such as those pertaining to such groups as the Crow, Polynesians and Ekoi, he attempts a "minimal" definition, one tending to isolate the lowest common denominators of all religious phenomena. He presents his picture as being provisory and precarious, affirming his skepticism regarding the adequacy of any definition that pretends to synthesize the totality of phenomena labeled as religion. The religious scholar is in this respect situated neither more nor less favorably than a biologist, whose research can certainly not be synthesized by way of a definition of Life.

In contrast with the opinion then prevalent, advocated most strongly by Wilhelm Schmidt, Lowie indicated the importance of animistic beliefs and beliefs relating to the dead in the religious complex of the Andaman, highlighting the difficulty of qualifying religious orientation as a whole in a monotheistic sense. Lowie also took part in the dispute over the notion of totemism, partly accepting Alexander Goldenweiser's theory on its origin as a phenomenon of "convergence." The theory intended to explain the existence of analogous or parallel phenomena in different parts of the world according to a convergent kind of evolution, said to occur within each single society in an independent manner: a theory to which Boas adhered as well. However, Lowie accentuates criticism of the very notion of totemism, stating that totemism does not exist as a fact per se, but is only the product of our system for classifying certain phenomena of primitive reality. (He thus anticipated Lévi-Strauss's criticism of the notion.)

In *Primitive Religion*, Lowie also deals with the particular concept of illness as *intrusion* of a material cause into the body of the ill person: a recurrent concept in the American and North Asian area. The foreign body could be introduced by an evil spirit, sorcerer, or enemy. Therefore the simplest form of therapy consisted of the extraction or "sucking" of the foreign body from the patient by special techniques, in particular the incision of the body part and clever exhibition of the object which the medicine man pretended to have extracted. In this regard Lowie observes that the principle according to which all diseases are things introduced into the body and capable of provoking violent reactions in it, was exceptionally widespread in North America, even though it had to compete with the differing concept of "soul-loss." The basic notion of illness, according to Lowie, was represented in America by the theory of "intrusion": i.e., the presence of a foreign body, which must be sucked out in order to cure the patient. The theory of "soul-theft" or "soul-loss," instead, refers to a later cultural stratum which, in some territories, had been superimposed on the archaic one. Taking up an idea previously formulated by Tylor and developing it in his own way, Lowie notes that the diffuse presence of the system of sucking, and the concept of illness as "intrusion" outside America as well, probably proves its ancient origins, datable back to the Paleolithic Age. Born in the Eurasian world, the concept was probably brought by the earliest immigrants to America. Therefore the comparative analysis of American and Siberian diagnostic and curative methods, with the presence in both areas of the method of sucking and the idea of soul-loss, leads us to recognize the existence of a single cultural matrix.

In *Primitive Society*, Lowie also analyzes the problem of "secret societies," a topic which had been discussed previously, in particular by Heinrich Schurtz, Hutton Webster, and Arnold Van Gennep. Lowie partly accepts Schurtz's hypotheses (*Altersklassen und Mannerbunde*, 1902), especially with respect to the gregarious or associative instinct with its evolutionary-psychological character. In part, however, he modifies the hypotheses, opting for suspension of judgment on several points while awaiting new interpretations. In his general conclusions he is careful to point out the harmful effect of the generic term "association" in reference to the numerous primitive societies. The division of an entire male society into groups of non-initiated boys, bachelors, and elders is one thing, he says; quite another thing is the division according to age groups of the Hidatsa Indians, or the division of Crow Foxes into youths, middle-aged men and elder members. It is probable that a nomenclature uniformly applied by us (that is, with terms such as "age groups," "associations," "secret societies," etc.) simulates analogies that do not exist in reality. By way of a brief analysis of the structural and cultural differences of several secret societies, Lowie arrives at a strong criticism of Schurtz's ideas on the unilinear evolution of associative facts. It is possible to say, he adds, that in all kinds of communities, the gregarious instinct is affirmed in one way or another; but this principle is only of a sociological order, and does not imply a theory proving the schematic and evolutionary succession of facts, whereas only an intense ethnographic study in every cultural area can establish the real sequence of developmental stages in associative forms.

It is not hard to recognize in these assertions of Lowie's the influence of Boas, whether in relation to unilinear evolutionary hypotheses, to the need for intensive ethnographic study of single phenomena, or finally, to the possible errors induced by the use of a generalizing nomenclature rather than a specific one for single phenomena.

In *Primitive Society* Lowie also deals with what he calls the dichotomy between the sexes, dedicating a chapter to the condition of women in primitive society, in which he once more stresses the fact that economic conditions are not always the factor determining the more or less inferior status which women occupy. For example, Lowie observes that among the Hottentots, pastoral life and sexual equality harmoniously coexist, while among the nearby Bantu, where women cultivate the land, they remain in a position of inferiority. Having discussed the age-old question of the condition of women in matrilinear societies, emphasizing that every case we know proves beyond the shadow of a doubt that nowhere is it possible to find a genuine matriarchy, Lowie (showing a sensitivity rarely shared by scholars, until then) also hints at the tabooization of menstruation as a possible factor in the prohibition against women participating in collective life. The monthly isolation of women—he says—has been considered one more proof of the state of degrading humiliation reserved for them in primitive communities; but it is highly probable that the causal sequence should be inverted. That is, the exclusion of women from certain social spheres and their consequent lesser liberty are probably the fruit of that sacred fear aroused by the recurring monthly phenomenon.

It is clear, then, that Lowie's work embraces all the major fields of interest and controversy in anthropology at the time. Frequently, it offers a new vision of phenomena, in that rigorous spirit of research which—though sometimes hampered by Lowie's passion for certain ideas—is nonetheless clear in its self-awareness, and unable to erase that indelible, implacable mark left by Boas's method.

Bronislaw Malinowski

Malinowski's personality was markedly different. An extraordinarily eclectic, sensitive observer of primitive society, he was born in Cracow, Poland, in 1884 and died at Yale in 1942. Because of World War I he remained for two and a half years in the Pacific islands, particularly in the Trobriands, which became his specific field of research. His books have become famous, partly because of his capacity to describe all the forms of behavior he observed through detailed analyses, rich with fondness for the peoples he encountered, while personally taking part in the life of the natives. Malinowski dealt with nearly all the most important problems of anthropology; in fact, he is something of a pioneer in more than one area: the linguistic one (as mentioned earlier), the economic one, the juridical, and that of sexual customs. Although his work as a field researcher is much richer than his theoretical work, Malinowski did attempt to formulate "laws" of cultural life, which he delineated in various essays, later collected in *A Scientific Theory of Culture*, published after his death in 1944. His hypotheses on the origin and function of culture arise above all from a strongly-felt need to react against the historic-cultural school of Schmidt and the attempts that had repeatedly been made, up to the early years of the 20th century, to reconstruct the evolutionary phases of cultural development. The "new science," says Malinowski, was born under the star of the most enthusiastic evolutionism, of anthropometric methods and prehistoric discoveries. It is not surprising that its earliest interests were concentrated around the reconstruction of human beginnings, the search for the *missing link* and investigations into the correlation between prehistoric facts and ethnographic data.

But Malinowski is well aware that in writing of the scientific aspect of the study of humanity, the anthropologist has a difficult task, since he must define the relations actually existing among the various branches of anthropology, and he must determine the place occupied by anthropology in the vast category of humanistic studies. Indeed, he must reopen the old question over whether and in what sense humanism can be scientific.

He expressed his will to demonstrate that the real common ground of all branches of anthropology is the scientific study of culture. As soon as the scholar of physical anthropology recognizes that the "race is the way in which it acts," he will also admit that no measurement, classification, or description of a physical type has any relevance unless and until we can correlate the physical type with the cultural creativity of a race. The task of the scholar of prehistoric man and the archeologist is to reconstruct the full living reality of a culture which has passed from partial limited testimony to material fragments. Even the ethnologist who uses facts pertaining to the primitive cultures of today and to the more advanced ones, with the aim of reconstructing human history in terms of evolution or diffusion, can found an argument on good scientific data only by understanding what culture really is. Thus, continues Malinowski, the scientific part of all anthropological work lies in the theory of culture, with reference to methods of direct observation and to the meaning of culture as process and product (*A Scientific Theory of Culture*).

The fundamental problem of Malinowski's methodology is thus the definition of "culture," which is "an integral whole consisting of instruments and consumer goods, constitutional charters for the various social groups, ideas and arts, beliefs and customs." Whether we consider a very simple or primitive culture, says Malinowski, or an extremely complex and highly developed one, we find ourselves facing a vast apparatus, in part material, in part spiritual, with which people can solve the concrete, specific problems confronting them. These problems arise from the fact that humanity has a body subject to various organic needs, and lives in an environment which is its best friend, since it provides him with the raw materials for human labor, and also its most dangerous enemy, since it harbors numerous hostile forces.

Malinowski does not doubt that the theory of culture must take up a position regarding the biological realm. Human beings belong to an animal species; they are subject to elementary conditions which must be satisfied so that the group can survive, the race continue and all organisms function. But with its apparatus of manufactured objects and its capacity to produce and evaluate them, humanity creates a second environment. This artificial environment is actually culture itself, which must be continually reproduced and maintained. Thus a cultural level of life is formed, with which new needs are manifested and new "imperatives" or "determinants" are imposed on human behavior. The fundamental needs and their cultural fulfillment are thus joined by new cultural needs, which therefore impose a secondary type of determinism on people and society. Thus we shall find instrumental imperatives arising from activities such as the economic, the normative, educative, and political; and integrative imperatives such as knowledge, religion, and magic.

The conceptual instrument which Malinowski adopts in order to articulate his theory is *function* which, taken in its typically bio-physiological meaning, designates the activity performed by an organ to achieve the end for which it is destined—whether separately or in relation to the other structures of the bio-physiological complex to which it belongs. In this respect, function is also an organ's aptitude for achieving its end. Malinowski declares the functional unity of society, on the basis of which every standardized activity or belief is necessary to the entire social system. Moreover, every form or element of a given society performs a necessarily positive function; just as certain functions are indispensable for the survival of a society, certain cultural and social forms are indispensable for the performance of these functions.

The functional theory and the concept of function immediately ran up against a number of fairly harsh objections among anthropologists; on several occasions Malinowski himself tried to confute such criticism by further clarifying his concepts. The concept of function—he says—is primarily descriptive, and consists of considering the way in which certain means, forms of organization, customs, or ideas widen the class of human possibilities on one hand; and impose certain restrictions on human behavior on the other. In short, functionalism is the consideration of what culture is as a determining principle: i.e., as a force augmenting the individual and collective level of life. Malinowski observes that this could perhaps provoke the oft-repeated criticism that the function of a cultural phenomenon always consists of showing how it functions. As a judgment of fact, this criticism is absolutely correct. But as a methodological indication, he adds, it reveals the low level of epistemological intelligence existing among anthropologists. The functionalist, to take a simple example, will insist on saying that in describing a fork or spoon, we must also provide information on how they are used, what relation they have with manners, with conviviality, with the nature of foods and cooked dishes and with the disposition of banqueting apparatus such as tables, plates, napkins, and tablecloths. When an antifunctionalist responds that, after all, there are cultures in which people use neither spoons nor forks nor knives, and that therefore function explains nothing, we must simply indicate that in the eyes of the scientific thinker, the explanation is none other than the most adequate description of a complex fact.

The type of criticism made against functionalism—that it can never prove why a specific form of drum or trumpet, table object or theological concept is prevalent within a culture—derives from the pre-scientific search for first causes or "true causes." These can be seen most easily in the persistent search for "origins" and "historical causes," in the nebulous realms of the historical past or the beginnings of evolution, which are neither documented nor recorded, of a people that has no history and has left no trace of its preceding evolution. In reality, observes Malinowski, history explains nothing unless it can demonstrate that an historical event has had a full scientific determination, and unless we can demonstrate this determination on the basis of well-documented data. In ethnology and in history, all too often the hunt for "true causes" proceeds in the vague realm of hypotheses, since no documentation exists. Here, speculation can wander freely, unhindered by facts (*A Scientific Theory of Culture*).

Even though (as we shall see) the lack of historical research remains one of the gravest problems of functionalism, it is certainly easy for Malinowski to criticize those who hunt for "origins" understood as "true causes." This, in fact, is the true misunderstanding underlying most anthropological theories on the origin of culture: defending at all costs the "prime factor," more or less explicitly affirming, along with its chronological priority, its causality as well: not only originating, but indispensable and permanent. Indeed, this is an apparently scientific, but in reality "theological," way of establishing the "prime mover," the true and only mover of history. Marx's theory on the economic factor as the prime determinant remained entangled in this "mythical need" which entailed the unsolvable problem of the relation between structure and superstructure; unsolvable precisely because, sustained by the need for a "theological causality," it has been absolutized by the followers of Marxist anthropology into a rigid, dogmatic form that neither Marx nor Engels had in mind. Both Marx and Engels often went back to this point, attempting to accentuate the need to take into account the interaction between the economic base and the superstructure; but they had not considered their listeners' need for the "absolute"; a need which (contrary to what is often claimed) is not at all identifiable in the need to simplify or schematize history.

As mentioned earlier, in Malinowski's view the development of the series of secondary needs, or instrumental imperatives, gives origin to integrative values—ideas, faiths, moral rules—which have meaning only in relation to culture taken as an organic and functional whole. According to Malinowski, symbolism is indispensable in transforming a physiological impulse into a cultural value; symbolism emerges as the very image of human culture. Again, Malinowski here rejects the hypothesis that one can discuss the "origins." Symbolic communication implies the existence of a group, and the existence of a permanent relationship among its members. Any discussion of symbolism without its sociological context is futile, notes Malinowski, just like any claim that culture could arise without the simultaneous apparition of manufactured objects, techniques, organization, and symbolism. In other words, we can establish that the origins of culture can be defined as the concurring integration of various lines of development: the capacity to recognize instrumental objects, the appreciation of their technical efficiency and of their value—i.e., of their place in the intentional sequence—the formation of social ties and the apparition of symbolism.

The problem of whether or not to admit the existence of "conscience"—continues Malinowski, of "spiritual realities," "thoughts," "ideas," "beliefs" and "values" as subjective realities in the minds of other persons, is essentially metaphysical. No reason can be seen why such expressions which refer to one's own personal experience cannot be introduced, providing that in each case they are fully defined in terms of open, observable, physically acceptable behavior. The entire theory of symbolism, therefore, consists of the definition of a symbol or idea as something that can be physically catalogued, described, or defined. Ideas, thoughts, and emotions must be dealt with together with all the other aspects of culture, both functionally and formally. The functional approach allows us to determine the pragmatic context of a symbol, and to prove that in the cultural reality, a verbal act or any other symbolic act becomes real only by way of the effect it produces (*A Scientific Theory of Culture*).

In ethnographic observation, then, it is always possible—says Malinowski—to define the ideas, beliefs, and emotional crystallizations of a completely different culture with a high grade of precision and objectivity. By way of the symbolic function, a particular physical reality or form of behavior assumes a conventional value, so that any cultural formation can only be achieved in relation to a "symbolic communicability," which transfers physiological impulses into signs. Therefore, the symbolic function gives rise to systems of signs, gestures, and sounds as a primary form of knowledge, and thus gives rise to knowledge itself.

Knowledge leads to the formation of religion and magic, which thus belong to the series of integrative cultural values; they are symbolic responses to various primary and secondary needs. Malinowski claims that the primary origin of the religious experience is due to a realization of the precariousness of existence. Even though its knowledge grows, humanity becomes more and more aware of the fact that its desires are often frustrated, that its expectations are exposed to changes in reality, that unpredictable dangers always lie in wait. The magic-religious response is born, then, from the conflict between hope—man's way of configuring a positive expectation—and the anxiety accompanying the prediction of possible failure. The series of human needs thus sees the birth of a demand for existential stability, for security in one's presence on earth, as against the uncertainty deriving from a cognitive appropriation of reality (*The Group and the Individual*, 1939).

The cultural answer to the new need is found in religion and magic, which are thus included in the functionalistic system, and are justified as instruments created by cultural symbolism in order to solve a situation of conflict: to liberate humanity from anguish and offer hope. Knowledge, magic, and religion thus represent the highest derived or integrative imperatives of human culture, since, by removing the causes of conflicts and doubts, they become essential factors of ethical, spiritual and social integration.

In this respect, a primary outline of juridical anthropology emerges with Malinowski, since he tends to establish what ethical norms and customs uphold single societies, leading the group to comply with ethically established forms of behavior even in the absence of a true political organization or explicit legislative and coercive organisms. In *Crime and Custom in Savage Society* (1926), Malinowski, indeed, tries to explore the forces that lead to order, uniformity, and cohesion in a primitive tribe, in order to understand why rules of conduct, as harsh, bothersome, or unpleasant as they may be, are observed. Although the problem is immense, and Malinowski's interpretative proposal a bit too elastic to be taken into consideration in strictly juridical terms (that, indeed, is the main reason he has been criticized by anthropologists), certain of his observations and perceptions remain worthy of reflection. Malinowski maintains that in the Melanesian society of the Trobriands, juridical phenomena consist of a set of binding obligations, perceived as a "right" for one person and "recognized as an obligation" by another, on the basis of a "reciprocity" mechanism, guaranteed by their being "public" and therefore supported by the incidence of personal interests, by ambition and by vanity. The theory of "reciprocity," already highlighted by Marcel Mauss's famous essay, "The Gift" (and bound to appear later on in a rich series of ethnological studies right up to Lévi-Strauss), is adopted here by Malinowski as a basis for the bilateral nature of all social relations—made obligatory by the desire for prestige, and by respect and fear of public opinion. Perhaps it is superfluous to affirm—says Malinowski—that no man, however "savage" or primitive he might be, will act *instinctively* against his own instincts or obey *unconsciously* a rule that he feels inclined to evade or voluntarily break; he will not act *spontaneously* in a manner contrary to all his appetites and inclinations. The fundamental function of law, he notes, is to repress certain natural propensities, to restrain and control human instincts and to impose a non-spontaneous, constrictive form of behavior; to assure a type of cooperation which is based on reciprocal concessions and sacrifices for a common end. In order to fulfill this task a new force must be present, different from innate, spontaneous endowments. The Melanesians, adds Malinowski, undoubtedly have the greatest respect for their own tribal customs and for tradition as such. All the rules of the tribe, whether banal or important, pleasant or unpleasant, moral or utilitarian, are considered with reverence by the Melanesian, and perceived as obligatory. But the force of custom and the fascination of tradition would not be sufficient in themselves to contrast the temptations of appetite or desire or the dictates of personal interest. There are other rules, dictates, and imperatives that require and possess their special type of sanction, beyond any simple attraction exercised by tradition. The natives of the Trobriands, for example, must conform to a very demanding type of religious ritual, especially in burial and mourning. In addition, there are rules of behavior among relatives. Finally, we find the sanction of tribal punishment owing to the irate, indignant reaction of the entire community. In a Melanesian community this sanction protects human life, property and, last but not least, personal honor, just as it does institutions such as the chief's authority, exogamy, rank, and marriage, which play a very important role in their tribal constitution (*Crime and Custom*).

Other fundamental problems posed by Malinowski are those regarding the relationship between "science," religion and magic ("Science and Religion," 1930). According to Malinowski, an attitude which he calls "scientific" and a religious attitude exist simultaneously in the primitive mentality, as in any other cultural context. That philosophical and epistemological system which we define as *science* begins, says Malinowski, with the use of observations concerning the past, in order to predict the future. In this sense, the spirit and practice of science must have sprung up in man's rational behavior as soon as he successfully undertook to create, construct and develop culture. The production of fire, notes Malinowski, would never be possible unless general distinctions regarding material, gestures, and their coordination were maintained within conditions necessary and sufficient for the success of practical execution. Even in the most primitive situations we thus see the clear emergence of real, relevant factors in a certain process which we can consider as a minimum definition of science, because it invariably implies the existence of general laws, of a field for exercise or observation and verification of the scientific discourse through practical application.

Religion and magic, instead, are born when the scientific attitude fails, leading to an existential crisis. Science is incapable of controlling the unpredictable, destiny, or the beyond. It cannot even control the outcome of many of our useful actions and forms of behavior, for often, even when it manages to know them, it is not able to dominate them. Magic thus appears when humanity cannot control chance by way of science; it is thus a functional instrument which cooperates with science, and which finds its specific utility not only in resolving situations of conflict caused by the uncertainty of chance, but also in the transformation of an organizing force of society. The magician, in fact, becomes the group's natural leader, and is frequently transformed into a chief or king.

In *Argonauts of the Western Pacific* (1922) and *Coral Gardens and their Magic* (1935), Malinowski also sheds light on the economic importance of magic. The magic of gardens, for example, gives rise to a system of farming controls which leads to collective benefits; magic rites performed in the construction of canoes are analogous in function. Malinowski thus comes to define magic— even black or subversive magic—as the ritual act celebrated to reach a result which cannot be achieved by way of human effort not supported by help (*Culture as Determinant of Behavior*, 1936).

Finally, in Malinowski's opinion, religion consists of a system of dogmatic affirmations, ritual technique, and ethical norms and precepts. Each of these components has it own function. In the presence of conflict, dogma offers a scheme of existential security, and rite and morals assume the highly important function of social guarantee. In this perspective, in Malinowski's view, myth assumes a particular role, since it is considered a simple development of dogma; indeed, dogma cannot be expressed except in myth, which is a narration intending to establish a belief, to serve as a ceremonial or ritual precedent, to establish a model for religious or moral behavior.

Religion, then, according to Malinowski, is necessary for the average individual in order to surpass the lacerations of the destructive anticipation of death, misfortune, and destiny. It resolves these problems by encouraging a belief in immortality or in a peaceful dissolution of humanity in the universe or in reunion with the divinity. It is apparent here that Malinowski seriously underestimated the problem of religion, particularly by failing to understand the extension of the field of the "sacred"—which goes well beyond the fear of death—and the interrelation of all its phenomena. Even while realizing that, on the basis of the functional explanation which he himself hypothesizes, religion becomes an uneliminable cultural factor because death is uneliminable, Malinowski actually had a poor grasp of its importance. This is rather surprising for an anthropologist who worked in the field using an analytical capacity still considered exemplary. In his path Malinowski finds innumerable magic rituals, and a nearly limitless series of taboos, formulas, and sacred precautions; he describes them in careful detail. However, he is unable to make out the elements linking them, precisely because on the basis of his functional preoccupation, he has split off magic from religion, instead of connecting the magical function with the scientific one. Therein lies Malinowski's limit. He accepts the social and cultural reality that he finds himself facing without asking any questions that go beyond "function." This explains why Malinowski did not ask himself why that attitude which he calls "scientific" is nonetheless "frozen," and therefore not open to an accumulation of knowledge among the "primitive" cultures. Thus he renounced both the possibility of knowing its past and its duration, and of finding explanations for such a phenomenon in a field outside the culture being investigated. Such an explanation might well involve the nature of magic itself, for in magic, nothing can be changed in precepts or techniques; these are not held to be acquired, but rather "revealed" (just as myth often recounts), and predetermined *ab illo tempore*.

Strangely enough, in another sector of his research as well, Malinowski failed to ask questions. It is in precisely that sector which made him famous, and which he described in various essays, particularly in *Sex and Repression in Savage Society* (1927). Even while examining matrilinear society in the attempt to discover whether a Freudian Oedipus complex was present, Malinowski seems not at all surprised by the condition of women, which he discusses at length, tranquilly pointing out the authority of the "mother's brother."

He does not seem particularly struck by the problem of the "diversity" of female group life, its subordination, and the witchlike negativity of women, which he nonetheless encounters repeatedly (and describes in *Argonauts*)—though by now the "chapter on women" has become fairly common in anthropological literature. The theorem according to which "everything functions" is never so valid as in the area of the female condition, whose "functionality" can certainly not be doubted.

Therefore Malinowski's views, though rich with perceptions and contributions to anthropological theory, present wide gaps; even more important, they reflect the risks connected with an antihistorical position: one offering solutions devoid of weight, devoid of conflict. Cultures are understood by Malinowski as autonomous, isolated complexes, each one sustained by an internal determinism proper to it. They thus become organisms which are independent of one another. This situation gives rise to the idea of "incommunicability" between cultures; the impossibility of confronting them; and therefore, a theory which is later to be called "cultural relativism."

Alfred Radcliffe-Brown, who had begun his work as an ethnologist with a study set up on functionalistic premises (*The Andaman Islanders*, 1922), was induced by fear of "relativism" to open a dispute with Malinowski, and propose a functional method that did not exclude (at least not explicitly) the contribution of historical knowledge of cultures. But in reality, what distinguishes the structural functionalism of the British school from Malinowski's functionalism is above all the concept of culture. The objectification of structures is evident in Radcliffe-Brown's method, so that the problem of "meaning," or of what, ever since Boas's times, had been called "the native's point of view," could not be considered at all, which leads the structural functionalist to renounce history. That is the conclusion we must draw from what Radcliffe-Brown himself observes. If it is generally valid to declare that the main function of the ritual or ceremony consists of expressing, and so keeping alive, the sentiments necessary for social cohesion, notes Radcliffe-Brown, we can "explain" any rite or ceremony by demonstrating the sentiments it expresses, and how such sentiments are connected with the cohesion of society (*Method in Social Anthropology*, 1958).

It is evident here that the meaning of sentiment will be deduced by the anthropologist in conformity with the cohesiveness necessary for a social system, whichever that might be in time and space, and whatever that meaning might be as "lived" by the subjects. But it is also clear that Radcliffe-Brown does not need the concept of culture as a unifying principle in the study of a society, just as he does not need history. What he needs is only the "synchronic" study of functions and structures.

Naturally, no anthropologist denies the importance of history, but whatever his "rationalizations" are, the fact remains that Radcliffe-Brown, like all other structural-functionalists, renounces history because it is not necessitated by the method. A convenient "rationalization," one difficult to deny, was close at hand, as regards the primitive societies examined by social anthropology, notes the author, but there is no historical documentation. For example, we do not know the developments of the various institutions among the Australian aborigines. Anthropologists who conceive of their studies as historical research, abandon themselves to conjecture and fantasy, and invent "pseudo-historical" or "pseudo-causal" explanations. For instance, adds Radcliffe-Brown, we have had innumerable and sometimes contrasting pseudo-historical theories regarding the origins and development of the totemic institutions of the Australian aborigines. Such theories, in his opinion, are not merely useless, but worse. This does not mean a refusal of a historical explanation, but exactly the contrary. (*Structure and Function in Primitive Society*, 1952).

At any rate, as had occurred with the followers of Boas, whatever their declarations of principle might have been, scholars of the Anglo-Saxon school did not take advantage of historical sources even when they were available; nor did they exercise their imagination in the least to set their research moving along historical lines. They were content to point out the lack of documents. In reality, synchrony leads us to ignore what precedes in a structural study; if what prompted Radcliffe-Brown to neglect history was his concept of social structure, Malinowski was led to do so by the functional concept of culture. Radcliffe-Brown does not hesitate to claim that whatever cannot be done in a synchronic study is unachievable; it is impossible, he says, to reach causal explanations in anthropology that are not mere conjecture. In order to establish the reliability of such conjecture, he wrote, it would be necessary to know laws of social development that we certainly do not know, and we shall probably never know" (*Structure and Function in Primitive Society*). On his part, Malinowski demonstrates the same conviction when he affirms that the functional point of view does not eliminate an evolutionary concept of culture which is valid and circumscribed, but "in actual fact" it discourages any hope of providing an exact reconstruction of human development (*The Life of Culture*, 1927). On the other hand, Malinowski is led to do without history both because of the meaning which he assigns to "function" (which as such is always indispensable, and never a surviving remnant; therefore it can be studied at any moment in its "present," in its "current existence"); and because he increasingly tends to accept only the psychological meaning of culture, "the native's point of view" (as Boas had done). Thus he renounces a true objectification of the culture that he describes.

On the basis of the same functionalistic premises, the anthropologist Melville J. Herskovits came to completely formulate the theory of "cultural relativism," which assumed the impossibility of mutual understanding between cultural complexes. According to Herskovits, there is no objective moral order, no universal system of values which has any objective basis. That is, the cultural products which are values are seen as such only in the culture to which they belong. Every culture is therefore a closed world, separate unto itself, with its own measure and ethical order. Those who condemn or exalt the customs and values of other societies, says Herskovits, formulate irrational judgments because they refer to facts or aspects of extraneous cultures, cultures which are therefore devoid of meaning, in the eyes of those who judge them.

Judgments, in fact, are based on experience, and experience is interpreted by each individual in relation to his own acculturation.

On the basis of this theory, as president of the American Association of Anthropology, in 1947 Herskovits presented a recommendation to the Human Rights Commission of the United Nations, known as the *Statement on Human Rights*, in which he claimed: 1) that one develops one's personality through his own culture: Consequently respect for individual differences implies respect for cultural differences; 2) that the concept of respect for cultural differences finds confirmation in the recognition that there is no scientific technique for qualitatively evaluating cultures; 3) that customs and values are relative to the cultures to which they belong.

Herskovits's recommendation to the United Nations was not accepted, but the problem of the relativity of values remained one of the most hotly debated, lacerating dilemmas for the anthropologist in the field.

CHAPTER VI

The Field of Transcendence

The Dispute Over the "Soul" and the Evolution of Religion

The anthropologists' work has been deeply important in interpreting the entire area of the "sacred." On one hand, the concept of the "cultural model," understood as a global organic system, made it impossible to go on discussing single religions outside their cultural context; this impossibility ended up by throwing into crisis and nearly destroying a discipline like the history of religions. On the other hand, an analysis of the "sacred" in "primitive" populations succeeded in shedding light both on its importance as a concrete, determining factor of cultural behavior, and its extension to customs, habits, prohibitions and taboos—which suddenly became clear and comprehensible in our culture as well.

It is to Edward Burnett Tylor (1832–1917) that we owe the definition of "culture" to which anthropology usually refers to indicate its true birth as an autonomous discipline. Moreover, it is precisely in this way of conceiving culture that we can understand how Tylor came to be deeply interested in religion. In his work, *Primitive Culture* (1871), Tylor defines culture as "that complex whole that includes knowledge, art, morals, law, custom and any other capacity and habit acquired by man as a member of a society." Although this may still appear as a simple list of factors, nevertheless it is precisely in that "complex whole" that the force of the definition is concealed; the notion of "complex whole" allowed

Tylor to put aside any research on chronological priorities or on the importance of one cultural trait in relation to others, and so to perceive the interrelations that were to lead to the concept of "pattern." So it is that, on an equal standing with all other types of behavior, religious behavior came to the fore as well.

It is in *Primitive Culture* that Tylor proposes a new hypothesis on the origin of religion. On the basis of a prevalently ethnological analysis, Tylor claims that we can find the origin of religion in a minimal form, the belief in spiritual "beings" or "essences."

Primitive man, which evolutionism still considered a model of prehistoric man, perceives within himself the presence of an elementary vital principle, which he calls "soul." We find here a kind of "experience-knowledge" which man achieves through dreams, sleep, illness; that is, in all those situations in which the "soul" seems to distance itself temporarily from the body, or else when it wholly detaches itself in death. At this point Tylor seems to anticipate a Freudian type of mechanism, claiming that the notion of "soul" is "projected" outside the subject, giving rise to the notion of "spirit" as an autonomous reality, sometimes independent of the body and sometimes present in it. The "spirit" is thus attributed to animals, plants, and inorganic beings with a process of successive "animation." In reality, the "primitive" thus discovers his "potency," which he nevertheless experiences as something marvelously extraneous, superior, and mysterious. Potency thus appears to him as closely joined to the external world; this is understandable, for it is easier to imagine a superiority outside than inside himself. There exists in "primitive" man a unity of essence between inner and outer reality, between the ego and the outsider; man knows that his being, or part of his being, lies outside himself, since there is no fracture between the environment and the ego. According to Tylor, the religious experience then develops into polytheism, with the attribution of "spirit" to natural realities, which assume divine "forms." Thus we find the god of the heavens, rain, thunder, the various stars, the winds, etc.; and later, the attribution of "spirit" reaches out to a limitless number of other realities, such as the gods of death and tribal ancestors. This mechanism should not surprise anyone, for as soon as individuals search for mankind's potency more and more exclusively in the "soul" and in the "spirit," they are necessarily led to think that death, in definitely separating body and soul, is the moment of authentic liberation, the entry into potent life. This line of thinking was to give rise to the idea that the soul must be immortal.

Finally, humanity reaches monotheism, the assignment of the essential attributes of divinity to one god alone, excluding any other. The road leading to monotheism reflects various modes of mythical process: the elevation of one of the gods in the polytheistic pantheon to supreme god; the formation of a divine hierarchy, in which spirits and other divine beings become figures dependent on a god considered as king or head of the pantheon; or finally, the ideation of a maximum divinity or "anima mundi" which gives potency to all the Universe and excludes any other representation of the divine. In this last perspective, monism and pantheism thus take shape again, and every object becomes a bearer of potency in virtue of the divinity inherent in it.

A similar theory had already appeared approximately a century before Tylor, in *L'origine des dieux du paganisme* (1767), by Nicolas Sylvestre Bergier. He claimed that fetishism and star worship arise from an infantile mental picture of natural objects as beings animated by genies and spirits. But evidently (and here we recall Kroeber's well-known premise that no new idea can be accepted unless the culture has reached the necessary maturation) the times were not ripe enough for Bergier's hypothesis to be received.

The form of animism proposed by Tylor, instead, enjoyed a great deal of fortune, because in establishing successive phases of religious development, it was in harmony with the scientific evolutionism of the late 19th century, even though Tylor himself had partly freed himself from a rigid evolutionary scheme.

Furthermore, this period saw the birth and growth of scientific psychology, which dealt with the problems of perception and the higher cognitive processes. It is not surprising that Wilhelm Wundt (1832–1920), one of the major psychologists of the era and the one closest to the problems of cultural and social psychology, was interested in Tylor's animistic theory, especially as regards the process of "projection." In his great work *Volkerpsychologie* (1905–1909), Wundt claims that the primitive (like archaic man) projects his ego onto the object by way of experience and apperception. However, partly modifying Tylor's theory, Wundt maintains that among the primitives there are two types of soul-representation. The body-soul, he says, is directly joined to the body and its organs; or rather, it is the life principle that the body carries within itself until death. The soul which separates from the body, instead, is a principle independent of it, and is designated as the *psyche*.

Many authors—historians, ethnologists, psychologists, philosophers—then threw themselves into the dispute over the concept of the soul, attempting through animistic theories and the spiritual world that gradually came to light among the "primitives," to understand not only primordial man, the moment of the "origins," but above all, our own spiritual world. These discoveries led to research regarding religion in the Old Testament, in classical antiquity, and in Germanic culture.

We can discern here the important role played by ethnological knowledge, once it had passed from the descriptive phase to the interpretative one: once it had finally come to pose questions about European civilization as well, no longer fearing to compare it to primitive cultures. Admittedly, monotheism was still seen as the ultimate, most advanced phase of the religious process; but the fundamental step had been taken, now that Tylor had considered and seriously analyzed all those beliefs and forms of behavior which previously had been put aside as incomprehensible, because they were completely irrational and devoid of true religious content. Arguments for and against Tylor's animistic theory went on at length, with varying outcomes. Emile Durkheim, for example, while giving Tylor merit for having freed the notion of "soul" from the philosophical premises considering it an immediate donnée of awareness, and for having finally considered it as a product of history and mythology, nonetheless contested the animistic theory considering the soul separate from the body. In the primitive vision, indeed, there is no hiatus between the physical organs and the soul. According to Durkheim, Tylor's error therefore consisted in assuming the phenomena of dreams, death, vision, and so on, as crucial in giving rise to the image of "soul," whereas in reality, the contrary occurs. Death cannot explain the transformation of the idea of soul into spirit, because, in the primitive concept, the soul is bound to the body and grows old with it. Moreover, it is not certain that belief in the "spirits of nature" could have formed after belief in the soul.

Durkheim's observations brought the problem of religion's formation back to its basic point. It had been all too easy to pass from animism to "naturism": i.e., to suppose that the worship of divine beings had arisen from the personification of natural forces. True, late 19th-century scholars were generally induced to consider religion as a manifestation of human creative fantasy, stimulated by the spectacle of natural phenomena. The poetical experience of our culture induced them to assume an attitude of this kind. Language itself (above all, poetical language), in conceiving natural phenomena as acts, seems to assume that those phenomena are backed by an *agent*. Do we not say that the sea swells, that lightning flashes, that the wind roars? Perhaps a kind of "language malady" has driven people to take these expressions literally, when they were only meant as images. Thus anthropologists were all the more prone to believe that the "primitives," reflecting on the causes of natural events, had invented gods, spirits and demons as the creators of all natural phenomena. Durkheim himself believes that religion might be "an immense metaphor devoid of objective value." But the crucial point touched on by Tylor could no longer be canceled: i.e., it was through introspection that primitive or primordial man came to conceive an early nucleus of religion having a soul-concept. By now, the idea was clearly emerging that "potency" and therefore, transcendence, exist within man; it is man who perceives it, intuits it, experiences it—though not in full awareness—within himself, inside himself. The fact that he finds potency and transcendence once more outside his being, in things, in nature, is only a way of evading this reality and, at the same time, explaining it. The mechanism of "projection," which had been adopted by Tylor, Wundt, and many of their followers, reemerged in Durkheim. While Durkheim, in opposition to Tylor, declares that the notion of "spirits of nature" might have preceded that of "soul" and that, at any rate, the notion of soul involves not a "chronological secondariness" but a "logical secondariness" (*Les formes élémentaires de la vie religieuse*, 1912), at the same time, he reproposes Tylor's strongest point: that is, the problem of "potency." According to Durkheim, through the formation of a group, the "primitives" (and analogously, all men) project "potency" onto a collective ego that transcends and surpasses them. Religion is none other than an image of power, of the transcendence of society. In spite of the contrast between Tylor's position and that of Durkheim, the central idea for both—no longer avoidable, because it allows us to understand the most varied cultural manifestations—is that of the "potency" and "transcendence" of man. It is man who is potent, and who looks for confirmation of his potency even while fearing it, by assigning it to nature, to things, and to the gods.

The Problem of "Potency": Taboo and Mana

The debate over religion among the primitives, and therefore, over the origin of religion itself, gave rise to numerous problems which cast doubt on notions held to be obvious until then. First among these was the idea of "nature" in relation to man. The notion of nature as something distinct, somehow opposed to culture, is very recent. It arose through the discovery of that equally "natural" environment for man—an artificial one constructed by man himself—which is *culture*. Before Rousseau, and the Romantic movement that followed him, man did not have a clear-cut awareness of the man-versus-nature dualism. It was with anthropology, the encounter with ethnological cultures, that the problem of defining nature began to emerge: no longer in relation to the universe as a "given," but in relation to the artificial man created by that second nature which is culture.

True enough, grief over human alienation from nature had often been felt in the classical world, and during the long journey made in time by Christian Europe; after all, the very idea of "progress" entailed the question over whether progress meant returning to an original state of Goodness, or else distancing oneself from a wild, beastlike state. But the totally new element emerging with the birth of anthropology (for good reason, Lévi-Strauss recalls it in his praising of Rousseau as founder of anthropology itself) is the sense of an opposition between nature and culture; or rather, the awareness that nature is not a "given," but a dominion constituted by man and transformed by his activity. This is a major subject of argument among psychologists, ethnologists, religious historians, and anthropologists. Their disputes and misunderstandings find a convincing explanation in humanity's radical fear of discovering not only its solitude in the world, but also its opposition to the world entailed by its very "potency." In this respect, suffice it to recall the attempt made by Lucien Lévy-Bruhl, with his theory on "mystical participation," to explain the experience that primitives have of nature and their surroundings (*L'expérience mystique et les symboles chez les primitifs*, 1938). This attempt aroused such lively debate that Lévy-Bruhl himself was induced to attenuate and modify his first hypothesis (in *Les Carnets de L. Lévy-Bruhl*, 1949). Mystic participation—that is, the sense of communion with things, with other men, with the gods—is not a prelogical form of thought in the sense that it precedes logical thought chronologically as a phase of development; rather, it is an essential component of that perception of one's own "potency," and of the will to find it again outside oneself, distinguishing human behavior in the most diverse cultures. In other words, mystic participation is not due to the incapacity to objectify external reality, nor is it a constant "psychological illusion" of primitive thought, says Lévy-Bruhl.

It was easier to perceive among the *primitives* this particular image of oneself and the world: this true *need* to seek a "potent" contact outside oneself through intercommunication, exchange, reciprocal gifts, and "sacrifice" which at the very moment of actuation give rise to a state of greater "potency." That was chiefly because ethnologists viewed the life and customs of primitive peoples with the distance and detachment of those convinced they are completely different from the objects of their inquiry. With their imposing capacity to fascinate, Lévy-Bruhl's early hypotheses aroused responses of whole-hearted acceptance, and then of refusal, because—together with the hypotheses of Tylor and Wundt—they shed light on one of the most important mechanisms informing all cultures, both as to individual psychological structure and social life. All the anthropological studies which followed ended up by redefining forms of exchange, communion, gift-giving, and sacrifice, which went beyond the limits of religion or religions, moving within that much vaster area which we are used to designating as the field of the "sacred." Today, we should finally be able to recognize its presence in an immense range of psychological, social, and cultural forms of behavior which no longer have anything to do with the supernatural, nor with the divine, nor with the existence of a God or gods. The "potent" man, bearer of potency, *passes his germ* onto everything that comes into contact with him; he thus individuates the presence of benign or evil "powers" in what surrounds him—in other men, other groups; in those who are different from him and in those who are to resemble him. This world of transcendence that man perceives in himself and projects outside himself thus gives rise to all those phenomena that anthropologists have studied and described; though they still have not managed to organize the mountain of data accumulated into a single, vast system founded on the potency and "transcendence" of man.

We can, then, list and study all the issues confronted by ethnologists, anthropologists, and religious historians; in the end, we shall find a factor unifying them and, at the same time, rendering them more obscure and mysterious: the problem of "potency." Monotheism and polytheism, prayer and sacrifice, taboo and mana, myth and worship, sacred and profane; but also exchange and alliance, sexuality and food, word and magic, today appear as phenomena totally interrelated to each other; they are pierced through and sustained by that dimension which people perceive in themselves, while at the same time projecting and adopting it, which we call "potency." It remains most difficult to define and delineate.

If we take up the trail cut by anthropology in the area of the sacred, once again we find ourselves facing the dispute over the evolutionary phases of religion, and the old argument over the origin of *monotheism*, which had been partly stirred up by Tylor's theories (for this reason, Raffaele Pettazzoni considers him the initiator of the history of religions as a separate discipline). Points in the dispute had already appeared toward the middle of the 18th century in the works of David Hume (*The Natural History of Religion*, 1979). He held that the original state of religion was *polytheism*—founded not on reason, but on the emotional aspects of humankind, continually prey to hopes and fears that end up being identified with divinities.

As mentioned earlier, in 1760 Charles de Brosses (1709–1777) published his book *Du culte des dieux fétiches, ou Parallèle de l'ancienne religion de l'Egypte avec la religion actuelle de la Nigritie*, in which he, too, maintained the existence of a primary stage of religion, the belief in a multitude of demons and spirits; only the Judaic religion, he said, developed without it.

In the area of 19th-century evolutionism, monotheism was once more viewed as the final, most perfect phase of different religious experiences. Comte, Lubbock, and Spencer followed one after the other in this dispute. Though each one saw the passage between various stages somewhat differently, all of them considered monotheism as the ultimate goal of the historical development of religions.

A scholar of Tylor's school, Andrew Lang (1844–1912), participated in the debate over the origin of monotheism. He based his hypotheses on the ethnological research carried out among the Australian aborigines by Alfred William Hovitt. Lang denied that monotheism could have developed from a preceding animistic phase, thereby refuting Tylor's theories; he also overturned the way in which the problem of evolution had been presented until then—i.e., as a gradual passage from rough, indistinct phases of religiosity to more and more mature, enlightened phases, finally blossoming into monotheism. Lang, instead, held that the idea of God is present among the primitives because religion is a fact inherent in human nature, even though mythological elements of greater or lesser rationality can subsist among the primitives. Such elements may develop over different periods of time (*The Making of Religion*, 1898). This position also underpins Wilhelm Schmidt's theory on *primordial monotheism*. It is true that the historic-cultural school born with Schmidt refuted the fundamental thesis of evolutionism intended as successive phases of development, but without a doubt, Schmidt was influenced by the biblical theology of a direct revelation from God to primordial man. He sought confirmation for it in the ethnological material available to him. Belief in a Supreme Being, said Schmidt, was present among all the primitive peoples, and our ancient ancestors left testimony of the primordial revelation in the various myths of creation which so many ethnologists have collected (*Der Ursprung der Gottesidee*, 1912).

It becomes clear here that historic-religious research, even while continuing to adopt ethnological material, now abandoned Tylor's main point of force—that is, an understanding of the religious phenomenon within the context of a set containing other cultural phenomena as well. At the same time, religious historians came to the fore who—unlike the anthropologists—did not try to free themselves of their own culture and the values established by it, but analyzed religious phenomena with a "theological" mentality. On one hand, they tried to fix the moment of the "origins" as one indicative of a religion's value; on the other hand, they tried to discern all those aspects—faith, prayer, rites, and worship—characterizing the Judaic-Christian religion. Such aspects were assumed as sure models of reference in order to evaluate "primitive" religions. Scholars thus tried to place "prayer" on the evolutionary scale in an effort to distinguish it from magic, or to establish its place in a chronological sequence in the conviction that the true, most perfect religion is one in which prayer expresses a personal relationship with the divinity—prayer devoid of magic gestures, and reflecting the human creature's attitude of obedience and trust. In such a framework we find Alfred Vierkandt, who held that all forms of prayer descend from an initial verbal form of magic; while Wundt maintained that in a primitive phase of religion, expressions of prayer are lacking because there are no personal gods to pray to; there are only magic formulas of invocation. Konrad Preuss assumed the same position; he, too, maintained that "religion of prayer," as humble, obedient abandonment to the divinity, can only come *after* a religion founded on magic ceremonies. The tendency of religious historians seems quite clear here, once they had distanced themselves from cultural anthropology. The problem of comparison was almost completely liquidated through an evolutionism which attempted at any cost to establish phases of development in which—explicitly or not—the Christian religion could be taken as a model. But most important, what these scholars failed to perceive was the central nucleus of a vast range of phenomena centering on the problem of "potency"; phenomena perfectly discernible even in the Christian religion and in our culture. This failure appears all the more surprising in that, during the same period, ethnologists and anthropologists were focusing on such potency-centered concepts and forms of behavior as "taboo" and "mana," which forced them to reconsider the mechanisms of magical thought. Nor must we forget that in the same years, Boas was urging everyone to abandon the theories and conjectures about the origins and phases of development of culture, and to start work not only in the "field," but also within the confines of each single culture, without prejudice and without any preliminary hypotheses.

Yet it is not difficult to understand the scholars' extreme reluctance to approach the area of the "sacred." For not only was the Christian religion held by believers and non-believers alike to be the highest expression of civilization; but above all, ethnological phenomenology brought to light the most secret and significant mechanisms of the area of the sacred, and thus of "potency," which had until then been hidden from our eyes, and experienced in an unconscious manner.

As noted earlier, this period gave birth to attempts to understand and explain such mysterious but widespread ethnological phenomena as taboos and mana. The term "taboo" had been known in Europe as early as 1784, the year of Captain Cook's account of his voyage to the Pacific islands. According to Cook, "taboo" has a very wide meaning; but it generally indicates things that are forbidden (and must therefore not be touched, for example). Later on, Christian missionaries identified "taboo" with "sacred"—i.e., "mana"—and this identification appears in complete form in a work by William Ellis, *Polynesian Researches* (1829). Ellis holds that "taboo" always expresses some connection with the gods, and that it therefore belongs to the area of religious meaning.

However, it was not till the early years of the 20th century that the phenomena of taboo and mana were proposed anew, as an important issue in the understanding of ethnological cultures. In this respect, James Frazer made an early attempt at systematic theory ("Taboo and Perils of the Soul," 1911), finding examples of taboos not only in all the archaic and primitive societies of America, Asia, and Africa, but also in the classic traditions and in European folklore.

According to Frazer, taboo is a mechanism meant to protect "potency" and to protect men from "potency." It magically renders objects and persons sacred, by isolating them for being sacred or impure. Both Mauss and Durkheim moved along similar lines; they, too, associated taboo with mana in a general attempt to reconsider the entire problem of magic: a problem centering on the hard-to-define but ever more pressing concept of potency.

Furthermore, for Durkheim, the taboo as a mechanism for separation and prohibition serves to establish the opposition between sacred and profane, since "sacred" beings—and therefore, "potent" ones—are by definition "separated beings," and the reciprocal exclusion between sacred and profane is a defense against the contagion of the sacred. Later, taboo was studied by a number of scholars of varying formation and tendency, including, of course, Sigmund Freud. In 1913 he published his *Totem and Tabu*, opening the way for a series of psychological, psychoanalytical, and psychiatric analyses on the topic. Above all, Freud stressed the ambivalence, the ambiguity, and the phenomenon of attraction-repulsion characterizing tabooistic behavior.

During the period in which research on taboo was being enriched, taboo was often linked with mana, a term gleaned in the Polynesian area in 1814 by W. Williams, who translated it as "power," or "influence." It was only much later, in 1891, with Robert Henry Codrington's *Melanesians*, that the term "mana" became very widespread in the sense of "supernatural force": A power distinguished from physical energy, capable of producing good and evil, it can be transmitted to every object and every man; spirits and souls separated from the flesh possess it and can pass it on. The notion of mana was later found in other areas, as the basis of magic; and the term was used more and more frequently in the sense of "power," generically understood as strength in relation to the supernatural. With Konrad Theodor Preuss, Robert Ranulph Marett, and John N. B. Hewitt, from the early 20th century onward, "mana" was conceived as a universal category, discernible in the most diverse ethnic areas (Hewitt, indeed, traced it down among Amerindians, who called it "orenda"). It always indicates a type of "primary potency"—a magic, religious power—wherever its efficacy can be conceived as automatic, or deriving from the nature of the person, or of the sacred object.

In this sense, taboo and mana are correlated. Taboo, in fact, indicates the fear of mana, mana being the expression of "potency." At this point the category of mana as "potency" and of the taboo connected with it become indispensable for understanding a great quantity of cultural phenomena and forms of behavior, which not only go beyond the confined area within which ethnologists and historians have relegated religion, but also beyond the extremely vaster one of magic, or the "sacred" in general. It is true that Boas, in tracing down the concept of mana among the various terms used by Amerindians, still believed that mana designated a fundamental religious notion ("Religion," in *Handbook of American Indians North of Mexico,* 1910); and that Durkheim, on his part, in interpreting certain magic-religious aspects of Australian cultures, connected them to an anonymous, impersonal "force," or sacred potency. It is also true that René Hubert and Marcel Mauss indicated in mana, as an idea of force par excellence, a universal notion of the same order to which the notion of "sacred" belongs; and that Lévy-Bruhl finds in it those immanent forces which are the vehicle and instrument of mystic participation; but in reality, despite all these efforts to define and circumscribe "potency," it remains a category open more to perception than cognitive understanding. Above all, ethnologists and anthropologists were unable, through "potency," to surpass the dimension of the sacred and magical as a category founded on the supernatural, on the divine, on the spirits, on a god or gods; so that they ended up by boundlessly expanding its area, making it encompass all those phenomena in which they somehow discerned "potency" itself. It was this misunderstanding that led scholars more or less explicitly to consider the ethnological populations as immersed in the magic-religious dimension; and it was this same misunderstanding that prevented them from individuating the mechanism of "potency" in those structures and social norms which, even while lying before their eyes, their own cultural experience led them to call "secular." For the same reason, they again failed to perceive the extension of the mechanism of "potency" in their own culture.

This strange situation gave rise to that current of studies on European folklore, the so-called "traditional" or "subordinate" populaces, and "peasant" cultures in which the magic-religious aspect was most evident, making it possible to create comparisons with primitive cultures. Even where it is impossible to hide from oneself the analogies between societies of an ethnological level and Western societies, this direction of inquiry is a way of evading any true awareness and acceptance of the phenomenon. It establishes a "distance," even allowing the scholar to exalt the wealth, authenticity, and positive value of groups which are "folkloric," or "subordinate," or "peasant," or "traditional"—once it is certain that they are different from the persons studying them (and that it is well for them to remain so).

What phenomena and behavior forms, then, did ethnologists and anthropologists treat superficially, even while studying the problem of taboo and mana? The most evident, macroscopic fact, hardly touched by anthropologists, is the profound social dichotomy between the sexes—the tabooization of the female group— even though it is present in all cultures. True, we do find brief mention of the problem here and there and, in anthropological literature, the custom of writing a short chapter on the female condition in primitive societies gradually came into use. But those who read such chapters realize that they are often written unwillingly, in a superficial, detached way, with a repressed sense of irritation and a clear position of psychological defensiveness. In reality, the brief chapters were often spurred on by the turn-of-the-century debate over female emancipation raging in the Western world. But what strikes us most is that scholars express doubt and interrogation only in the terms with which such doubt and interrogation are expressed in Western society, so that they appear almost blind in the face of evidence. Almost nothing of the reality of women's life in primitive societies emerges as a problem in their eyes. For example, they do stop long enough to consider maternity as a fundamental value in archaic cultures; but it is certainly not this type of attention that can surprise us, given that maternity is a value in any case—even when subject to debate—in the scholars' societies as well. At the same time, these authors only hastily note the tabooization which accompanies women throughout life, from puberty to menopause, during menstruation, pregnancy, the postpartum period, and nursing. They seem to consider such tabooization a tiny detail, hardly worth their attention. Moreover, if we consider the great number of pregnancies, the taboo accompanying abortion and miscarriage, the lengthy nursing period, and the life expectancy of women in ethnological societies, which ran to around 35–40 years (meaning it generally did not surpass the menstrual cycle), we can only remain surprised by the scarce importance given by researchers to a tabooization which virtually made the female group a totally separate one. As we shall see more plainly in regard to studies on myth, women are totally separated, in an even more radical way than with taboo, in being excluded from initiation. But even this phenomenon failed to appear as strange; it has not been emphasized except parenthetically by anthropologists, though it clearly entailed that same ambivalent mechanism of exclusion which had been discussed in research on taboo and mana.

The researchers' undeniable blindness is surprisingly manifest in Malinowski, who nonetheless was most sensitive in his vision of the daily life, social structures, customs, and implicit and traditional norms of primitive cultures. Malinowski dedicated particular attention to the phenomena of taboos and magic, attempting to achieve a critical revision of them based on deeper analysis. Furthermore, he also investigated the sexual life, matrilinear societies, the concept of procreation and the emotional role of the child, but in spite of all this, he continually brushed up against the problem of women without perceiving it. In his revision of the taboo concept, Malinowski tried to clarify both the formation and functional nature of various taboos, distinguishing between those which are fixed and immutable and those which, instead, appear only occasionally in connection with particular social events.

In *Sex and Repression in Savage Society* (1927), Malinowski examines the taboo of incest in Trobriand society in an attempt to verify the substance of Freud's hypotheses on the Oedipus complex, which he had previously examined at length. He concludes that the incest taboo, like the various prohibitions that accompany sexual union and regulate it socially, is an effect of culture, which acts against an innate impulse and thus strictly separates man as the bearer of culture from the animal world. The incest taboo is seen by Malinowski, as by numerous anthropologists before and after (right up to Lévi-Strauss), as a surpassing of nature by culture. "We have succeeded in deducing the need for the incest taboo from the change in the endowment of instinct, which must proceed on the same level with the social organization and culture; incest as a normal type of conduct cannot exist in humanity, because it is incompatible with family life, whose very foundations it would disorganize." In this respect, then, Malinowski takes into account the incest taboo only in the restricted area to which we are accustomed: i.e., between parents and children, brothers and sisters; and he deduces a social norm that will prohibit it. Thus he does not confront what, in a psychoanalytic sense, is the paradigm of incest: that is, the mother-son relationship; nor does he consider the extension of taboo throughout the clan, in primitive society—that is, the institution of exogamy (though he does point out a tragic case of rupture, ending in the suicide of the "sinner," in *Crime and Custom in Savage Society*). But above all, Malinowski does not take into account the fact that the only true incest that actually occurs with some frequency in all society, including ours, is that of father with daughters in the nuclear family; while as far as we know, the type presented as paradigmatic, that of mother and son, never occurs. We thus find ourselves once more facing the fact that anthropologists have never made a clear inquiry into the condition of women; indeed, they have even looked at the female condition without seeing it. In this respect Lévi-Strauss's attitude is significant, both in his analysis of myths, and in that study on the Nambikwara which nevertheless is now considered exemplary in anthropological literature. (This fame also accompanies Malinowski's studies, which are just as short on analysis and interpretation of the female condition.)

In fact, Lévi-Strauss finds that the five-day prohibition against eating, to which Nambikwara women are subjected during the monthly cycle, is not harsh, because particular foods are often forbidden. It is surprising to hear that this prohibition is not considered harsh for a populace living on the edge of survival whose only food, during long periods of the year, consists of berries and other wild plants gathered by the women as they wander from place to place. It is all the more surprising in that, in his note accompanying the passage in question, Lévi-Strauss claims that in native women (as pointed out by other travelers and ethnologists), the menstrual flow is scarce or even, for long periods, absent. Naturally, it is hard to know whether this is actually true, given the taboo surrounding the phenomenon of menstruation and, therefore, the possibility that women used tampons made of plants, which the ethnologist might not have seen. At any rate, the most immediate, simple cause for the scarcity or even the absence of menstruation, now ascertained by numerous studies touching, in part, on the periods of famine in Europe, is insufficient nourishment. Lévi-Strauss does not consider this factor.

In any case, Lévi-Strauss notes, the Nambikwara men "treat

The Problem of "Potency": Taboo and Mana   127

their women with a great deal of affection and tenderness." He seems to nourish no doubt about this, though the men's opinion of women is openly revealed in their metaphysical convictions. After death, in fact, the men's souls will survive, because male existence is fertile and lasting, like agricultural life on earth; while women's lives, analogously with their nomadic existence in the arduous, scarce gathering of berries, "leaves no trace more durable than what their souls leave, which dissolve in the wind and rain" (*La vie familiale et sociale des Indiens Nambikwara*, 1948). This is one of the most poetic passages in Lévi-Strauss's study, but in its beguiling beauty, it unfortunately betrays the anthropologist's sympathy for the masculine values which he describes, and his incapacity to grasp the contradictions, conflicts, injustice, and abuses which most clearly flourish also in the marvelous world of the Nambikwara.

We find another highly indicative example in Malinowski's interpretation of taboo, in connection with the complex phenomenon of "kula" (*Argonauts of the Western Pacific*, 1922). Kula, very simply put, is a ceremonial, cyclical system of exchange representing a fundamental structure in the life of the Papuan-Melanesian populaces of New Guinea. According to Malinowski, the various tabooizing forms of behavior function as a guarantee against the risks that kula entails. For example, when the kula canoes set off for their ventures, the women, who "obviously" do not participate in the most important ceremony of society (Malinowski takes the fact for granted), may weep, but it is taboo for them to weep during the period comprising the navigation cycle, in which the men are far away. The men pass through a period of danger until they have terminated their tour of the islands and their series of exchanges. The question remaining is why their vital force and their probability of success should be endangered by the behavior of the women, who have remained at home. That is, we still must ask what the very essence of taboo is, and the concept of "potency" encompassed in it, in relation to women. Neither Malinowski nor other anthropologists stop to consider the matter in depth. In fact, Malinowski limits himself to stating that taboo is meant to temporarily deprive women of their essential functions, and to prevent them from performing acts which might weaken the power of males. But it is this very connection, which he takes for granted, that one ought to understand; this connection leads us to refer to a kind of "mystic participation," and thus to a particular mana in women, since the "function" is evidently not sufficient to explain the interrelations of the phenomena.

During the kula period, not only are women forbidden to weep, but they cannot leave the village alone, they cannot receive male visitors, and (perhaps it is superfluous to add) they must not have sexual relations. If a woman were to "misbehave," in fact, her husband's canoe would float along slowly, becoming subject to greater risk. Malinowski fails to note the most important factor: that is, how much women-centered taboos resemble each other, in the most varied cultures and areas, on the occasion of men's dangerous ventures. This factor leads us to suppose that the taboos regard not so much the risk of the kula's economic failure (which he emphasizes), as they do the risk for men themselves: a risk tied to the possession of women and to the certainty of this possession, especially in relation to men's sexual capacity and "potency," which may always turn out to be negative. The prohibition against weeping might best be explained in this connection, since in a great number of societies, the weeping of women is institutionalized in a ritual form connected with death and mourning.

We thus find ourselves once more facing the problem of "potency." In the case of kula, potency clearly resides in women: in their capacity to cause the death of those who, like the canoers, already run the risk of dying. But we cannot stop at this point to consider the connection between woman and death, for what must be stressed is that "potency" here is a declaredly human "force"; it does not spring from the supernatural or the divine, but "establishes" transcendence even while remaining in the ambit of the human. In fact, as appears with absolute clarity in all taboos regarding women, it is their human reality that includes the sacred. It is not the sacred which includes the human, for women are institutionally excluded from the sacred.

Hypotheses on Myth

In order to better understand the vast field of transcendence and the sacred, we must mention some of the studies which religious historians, ethnologists, and anthropologists have done concerning myth. This does not mean that myth has always been considered a factor pertaining to the sacred; indeed, myth has often been dealt with in the area of poetry, literature, and fantasy; it has been considered a form of thought more or less collateral to the sacred. But in a cultural analysis, the sacred covers an immense space precisely because it assumes dimensions and values which go beyond the boundaries of religion and magic, becoming the context in which man unconsciously objectifies his transcendence and power.

Toward the end of the 19th and the beginning of the 20th century, alongside studies on taboo, religion, and mana, we see an intensification of studies on myth. These studies drew enrichment from anthropological and ethnographic contributions. However, in spite of these efforts at achieving a deeper understanding, myth still remains one of the least comprehensible problems in the history of human societies. This leads us to suppose that scholars have placed it in an area and scheme which imprisoned it, preventing a plausible interpretation of it. If we quickly retrace the steps taken by the various historians and anthropologists who have been interested in myth, we find a series of hypotheses which, far from mutually excluding one another, illumine the various facets of myth, and all appear convincing to some degree. But we always end up finding ourselves facing something incomprehensible, or at least difficult to perceive, which we have trouble concretizing. Nor can we take refuge in the idea that we are dealing with narratives which—sacred or not, true or not—have no influence on real life. On the contrary, more often than it may appear, myth serves to establish and justify the institutions, customs, and values upholding the history of a people, or the story of a group belonging to a people. For example, who could deny the importance that the myth of Adam's temptation by Eve has had in the history of women, in Christian Europe? The female image, seen as the image of sin itself, led men to sculpt on the capitals of numerous cathedrals terrifying faces of women, symbols of desperation and condemnation, which they did not hesitate to inscribe simply as "diabolus." These faces are nothing other than infinite replicas of Eve, and therefore the symbol of woman herself. The horror felt for women throughout much of medieval culture can be summed up in the cry repeated innumerable times from Augustine onwards, "*Per feminam mors!*" It, too, sprang from the myth of Eve.

But of course, in spite of the enormous quantity of studies carried out on myth, the unanswerable question remains the same. What does myth narrate? An entirely interior, more or less conscious reality, or something which, though veiled and hidden, refers to a remote past? As we shall see, this question emerges repeatedly, though formulated differently by various scholars. It will remain without an answer until scholars try to proceed from myth to the most important query. Who invented, constructed, or narrated the myth?

In surveying the various hypotheses on myth and its function, we can doubtlessly discard that of Comte who, observing the usual law of evolutionary stages, attributes the mythological phase to a primordial stage of culture, characterized by a theological type of fantastic pretense. According to Comte, mythology must not be identified with true and proper religion, which instead develops during the last evolutionary stage, bringing full harmony of life, heart and intellect. Clearly, Comte's evolutionary thesis is amply disproved by the existence even today of religions founded on myth, such as the Judeo-Christian one, and by the wealth of mythologies in all cultures, whatever their form of worship.

According to Lévy-Bruhl, on the contrary, mythical invention represents the sacred "history" of inferior societies: a history dominated by a sensitive, mystical drift, entailing collective representations and tending to achieve communion with mystic reality in an emotional form. However, in the revision he made of his theory on prelogical thought, Lévy-Bruhl went back to this definition and asked in what sense one can consider mythical history to be "true." Myths are stories of what has really taken place in a time, space and world which, though real, are different from the present time, space and world. Myths are therefore revelations relating to an extra-temporal period, full of supernatural beings and events. The query emerging, then, is what must be intended as "reality" and—though not explicitly—we already perceive here a psychological dimension of mythical creation destined to reappear, though in different form, in the hypotheses of Wundt, Freud, and Gustav Jung.

The Italian scholar of myth, Raffaele Pettazzoni, follows a similar line. He refers to what Giambattista Vico said about mythopoeic fantasy as a function of the spirit, and stresses the autonomy and creative aspects of the interpretation of reality contained in myth. Pettazzoni was well aware of the importance of the problem of the "truth" and "reality" in myth; he therefore states that myth does not function as pretense or fable, but as true history, both in its contents (narration of facts which really happened in a condition which preceded and determined present reality) and in its sacredness, since it sets sacred forces into motion which are useful to the group through ritual ("Verità del mito," 1947–1948).

At this point of our inquiry into myth, two essential questions emerge: if myth narrates a true story, an event, why is this story a culturally "founding" one? And if myth is a creation of fantasy, if it is an artistic invention, then once again, why is it culturally "founding?" By "founding" we indicate that in all cultures, myths underlie powerful institution, such as initiations, religions, rites, ceremonies, sacred times, sacred spaces, feasts, prohibition, taboos, forms of sexual behavior and, above all, the strongest institution: the cultural dichotomy par excellence, the dichotomy between the sexes, with the subordination and social exclusion of women.

This is the very reason why we must ask *who* created myth.

Naturally, at a given point, research on the psychological foundations of myth appeared to scholars as indispensable. Vico had been the first to move off in this direction; his theories were taken up by Wundt, who maintained that myth was a product of the imagination, and belonged to a representational and sentimental world which he denominated "mythical apperception." However, Wundt did not hypothesize an autonomous mythopoeic function, and denied that myth contained specific elements of truth, since it is formed under the preponderant influence of emotion. The idea of a mythopoeical mechanism, he said, is based on misunderstanding, for the products of mythical apperception, subjective in themselves, take on the illusory appearance of objective perceptions, presenting themselves as immediate realities.

With these affirmations of Wundt's, we now find ourselves confronting the hypothesis of "projection." In Freud's view, of course, the content of the projection is filled by the subconscious; with the analysis of dreams, which became one of his most important instruments for the understanding of myths, a fundamental step was taken in the connection between psychoanalysis and anthropology; or better, between psychological structure and culture. According to Freud, through transferrals which one needs to interpret correctly, the dream translates the profound movements of the subconscious; for him, it becomes evident that the language of myths is analogous to that of dreams. It is therefore possible, he says, to decipher their particular symbolism. Myth is thus conceived as a highly elaborated collective manifestation of the human spirit, of which it reveals, and, at the same time, dissimulates certain subconscious tendencies. This would explain the sense of the Oedipus myth, for example, in which Freud thought he recognized the dramatic expression of a universal phase of humanity's psychic development.

Followed in this direction by his most famous students (such as Otto Rank, Karl Abraham, and Carl Gustav Jung), Freud attempted to discover the "forgotten language" of myths, while his "science of dreams" serves to reveal to ethnologists and anthropologists that the manifest content of a symbol or myth always covers a latent content, one not emerging at the conscious level. Jung in particular (1875–1961), though distancing himself considerably from Freud's views, accepted the fundamental notions of "unconscious" and "consciousness," as well as the technique for analyzing psychic phenomena (dreams, neurotic symptoms, etc.). At one essential point in Jung's theory of the "psychic," he confronts a problem we have often found ourselves facing in our studies of myth: that is, the content of "reality." In Jung's view, the *consciousness*, which forms the "psychic" along with the *unconscious*, is man's capacity to relate persons, situations and things to his ego. In other words, it is the individual condition for learning external reality, in its relation to the subject. Therefore, the contents of the consciousness are subjective. At the same time—and this is the point which most directly interests us—these contents constitute a subjective psychic reality: that is, a reality autonomous from any ontological value judgment regarding the actual existence of the object entering the area of consciousness. Jungian analysis, then, tends toward an investigation of subjective psychic realities which are based on an individual judgment of reality. However, the psychic reality is always objectified more clearly when a *consensus gentium* helps to define it: that is, the presence of the same learned notion or the same psychic attitude in a plurality of individuals. In myth, as in other particular states such as those of dreams, symbolic production and neurosis, what emerges from the unconscious and is somehow activated and actualized are the "archetypes," which are "constant forms," possibilities for representation, motives that reappear in similar form at all times and in all places (*Das Gewissen*, 1958).

This touches on one of the problems previously posed by various anthropologists: the similarities discernible in myths of different populaces living at a great distance from each other. True, Bastian had already complained of the "frightful monotony" of the fundamental ideas of men all over the world, and Boas used to say that nothing seems to travel faster and more easily than fantastic stories, given the hunger men feel for them and, at the same time, their laziness in creating them; which would justify the hypothesis of "transmission" explaining the presence of the same ideas in places distant from one another. On the contrary, Malinowski, as always concretely realistic, defines myth on the basis of function, as a story narrated in order to establish a belief, serve as precedent in a ceremony or ritual, or act as a model for moral or religious conduct (*Myth as a Dramatic Development of Dogma*). Thus, the relation of myth to social structures is multifarious, in the sense that myth justifies and determines certain actions (rites, for example) that tend to resolve moments of crisis; and it founds certain theoretical and moral truths which operate in guiding the group.

As regards the role of the unconscious in the creation of myths, Jung, too, refers to the presence of similar or even identical mythical elements among different peoples separated by enormous distances in space and time. As mentioned earlier, he notes that such elements present profound analogies with the spontaneous representations of dreams and other products of the unconscious. He is thus led to attribute them not to an experience originating externally, but to the archetypal function of the collective unconscious (*Wandlungen und Symbole der Libido*, 1912).

Within the Jungian school, the work of Erich Neumann enjoyed particular success precisely because of his use of myths. In *The Great Mother* (1955), he examines the "archetype" of maternity at various cultural levels. He points out that when analytic psychology deals with the primordial image of the Great Mother, it refers not to some concrete image existing in space and time, but to an interior image operating in the human psyche. The symbolic expression of this psychic phenomenon, says Neumann, is to be sought in the figures of the Great Goddess as represented in myths and artistic creations.

The term "Great Mother," adds the scholar, a partial aspect of the Female archetype, is a late abstraction which presupposes a highly developed speculative consciousness. The feminine archetype structurally contains a positive character and a negative one. The positive aspect entails manifestations of protection, nourishment, and generation by a female nature, while the negative one—evident in the typology of tremendous, destructive Goddesses—corresponds to the unleashing of unconscious, antimaternal male impulses.

In *Zur Psychologie des Weiblichen* (1953), Neumann describes a succession of phases in which the ego is liberated from the unconscious. At the end of the process, he writes, the ego finds itself at the center of the modern Western consciousness, confronting the unconscious as a psychic system distinct from itself. In this evolution leading to liberation from the dominance of the unconscious, the symbolism of the consciousness is masculine, whereas the symbolism of the unconscious, as indicated by mythology and the symbolism of the collective unconscious, is feminine, representing as it does the opposition against the emancipation of the ego.

At this point we must observe that Neumann is all too easy-going in disposing of the problem which such statements entail. In a note, he hastily adds that "masculine" and "feminine" are symbolic terms, not meant to be concretely identified with "man" or "woman" as bearers of precise social characteristics. He goes on to state that matriarchy and patriarchy are psychic stages characterized by a different development of the consciousness and unconscious. But aside from any other consideration, the scientific falsity of Neumann's method is palpable. He repeatedly refers to the work of Bachofen who, in the burgeoning of evolutionary anthropology during the 19th century, claimed the historical reality of a period characterized by the empowerment of women: basing his opinions not only on myth, but also on a set of religious, juridical, and social phenomena which he denominated as "matriarchy." The only historically certain element in this whole set of factors is the cult of the Great Mother, which Neumann, instead, hastens to define as an "archetype," above and beyond any historical concreteness. At the same time, however, he defines a supposed set of forms of behavior, hypothesized by Bachofen as the historical period of "matriarchy," as a "psychic stage." The distortion of Neumann's scientific method becomes patent here. It results from having interpreted data historically present in various cultures on the mythical, religious, or artistic level, as evidence of psychic structures; and then, from having completely abandoned any historical reference for structures in which time and space are submerged and annulled. In this manner, it is impossible to break a vicious circle in which, in order to prove the existence of the psychic stage, one takes up certain historical facts; and in the absence of other historical facts, states that what we have is only a "psychic stage." But Neumann actually presupposes a true and proper historical development of the "consciousness," established in Western culture and relative to the male group alone.

In *Zur Psychologie des Weiblichen*, he states that "matriarchy" does not signify only the dominance of the archetypal Great Mother, but an overall psychic situation in which the unconscious (and femininity) dominate, whereas the conscious (and masculinity) have not yet reached autonomy and independence. "Patriarchal," he adds, does not indicate the sociological dominance of the male, but rather the predominance of a male consciousness which has succeeded in achieving the separation between the systems of the conscious and the unconscious, and which has become quite solidly established in its opposition to the unconscious and in its independence from it. Modern woman must therefore also pass through all the stages of development leading to the formation of the patriarchal consciousness—the one dominating patriarchal culture and, indeed, Western consciousness in general.

At last, then, an investigator of myths—fortunately free of racist preoccupations—decides here to declare that the unconscious is feminine; that this unconscious predominates both in prehistoric times and in the phase ontogenetically corresponding to infancy; and finally, that even today women are dominated by the unconscious, and so have stopped at the beginning of the formation of consciousness. Only at this point can we attempt to answer the basic question. Who created myth? If, as mentioned earlier, myths underlie extremely important institutions such as initiation, from which women are always excluded, religions, taboos, and virtually the entire social organization, which myths justify and guarantee, then we must answer that myth is a creation of the male group. The reason, indeed, is quite simple. Why should women have excluded themselves from the most important institutions of society by way of myth? Why should they have taken on the burden of the most tremendous sins, such as having introduced death into the world? Why should they have described their physiological impurity? Why, their own "potency" as negative? And above all—in all the studies on myth—why have anthropologists, historians and psychologists wavered between attributing myth to a generic collective unconscious, and to the creative fantasy of the group, never noticing that in reality, the only *active* group, using myth to explain their origins and justify their power, is the male group? The only theory offering us the possibility of deducing such a fact—that myth sprang up as a male narrative—is Freud's theory relative to the killing of the father by the male sons, in order to ensure possession of women in the primitive horde. As is well-known, according to Freud, the destiny of this horde and its sense of guilt have left an indelible mark on the human heritage, in the prohibition against eating the totem animal (a substitute for the father devoured by the son in the primordial drama), and in the prohibition against incest. We might therefore hypothesize that an entire series of cultural institutions and creations, including myth, must have been dictated by the male unconscious, since the primitive act took place among males. However, Freud never said as much.

No scholar of myth has ever brought to light this aspect, even when (as in the case of Lévi-Strauss) he found himself confronting a great quantity of myths dealing with the symbolic meanings of women, the origin and establishment of norms weighing heavily on them, and the function that they are called upon to perform as an instrument of counterweight and defense for males, who are the creators of culture as opposed to nature. True, Lévi-Strauss states that myths "have no author: whatever their real origin, from the moment they are perceived as myths they do not exist unless they are incarnated in a tradition" (*Le cru et le cuit*, 1964). But (aside from the fact that, since myths concretely exist, someone—

whether an individual or group—must have created them) what counts in Lévi-Strauss's statement is that the force of myth lies in its being perceived exactly as "myth": that is, as word-act, as a "potent" word, as a foundation of a reality which men are obliged to live. Therefore, without pretending here to sum up the complex structural method Lévi-Strauss used to analyze South American myths, it is impossible to avoid marveling at the fact that one of the greatest researchers of myth was not struck by their patent male origin.

Of course, such an affirmation, in the context of the structuralist theory, would lead to grave conclusions: i.e., that the masculine "type of thinking" is different from the feminine, since for Lévi-Strauss what counts in the analysis of myths is not the content, but the way in which thought functions. And yet this observation fades into the background if we reflect on the fact that even the creation of myths is a way of "attacking reality," a system for explaining reality; whereas it is this—the possession of reality by its theorization—which has been denied women, at all times and in all places. In Western culture they have been kept from access to philosophical, theological, and scientific knowledge—the very type of thought exercise which leads to the possession of cultural reality—even while being forced to live out its consequences. In ethnological cultures they have been denied access to initiation, and to knowledge of the group's myths (which are transmitted under obligation of secrecy to candidates for initiation), even while being obliged to accept and live out the myths' meanings.

At any rate, the fact remains that, by adopting the contents of the myths alone, one could construct a complete system of the place and function assigned to women in culture. This would arouse great unease and a sense of helplessness in any reader prone to denial. In fact, as Lévi-Strauss affirms, "not only are myths, like rites, *in-terminable* ... but music [according to the analogy established by Lévi-Strauss between musical and mythological structure] and mythology set man face to face with virtual objects of which only the shadow is real, with conscious approximations to truths which are inevitably unconscious" (*Le cru et le cuit*).

In summing up the path we have attempted to trace in the extremely vast area ranging from prayer to rite, from taboo to myth, and from magic to religion, I think we can conclude that man, by weaving a thick web of interconnections between meanings and forms of behavior, and between actions and symbols, in that global context which we have called "culture," experiences his own "potency" and projects it onto a transcendence which, in being objectified, appears to him as a reality surpassing him and driving him. The first attempt made to somehow bring this "force" from outside, where man had projected it, back to man's inner self, was probably the one performed by Freud. In adapting in a Freudian sense the oft-repeated saying of Augustine, we could affirm that *"in interiore homine habitat veritas."* If truth does live inside man, then no taboo makes sense. For nothing outside of man can contaminate him, just as no sacred time and no sacred space is more powerful than man—who, instead, establishes them, respects them, and fears them.

Is it perhaps indispensable for man to set up a "distance," a "difference" between himself and his self—to objectify his reality in order to understand it? And has woman been overcome by man so as to represent the first and fundamental "distance," the first and fundamental "difference," symbolizing and, at the same time, incarnating all others?

CHAPTER VII
Psychology and Anthropology

Psychology and Culture

It was Lévi-Strauss who stated that ethnology is, first of all, a "psychology." To what degree is this true? The object of ethnology's inquiry is the study of cultures, and in the early days, as we have seen, this meant studying cultures from outside, as if they were things; and in describing them just as they appeared to the observer, with the greatest honesty possible. Culture was thus perceived in its external forms: in forms of behavior learned by the individual as the expression of an ethnic group and therefore different from one group to the next. At the same time, the early travelers, such as missionaries and ethnologists, were basically convinced that these differences were at any rate dictated by the psychic and physical constitution of individuals as members of a race and—though in an obscure way—the customs of a people were held to be specific characteristics of the single members of that people. The problem of a duality between psychology and culture was to progress only gradually, precisely because neither the principles of an individual psychological structure nor those of a possible global internalization of culture had yet been sufficiently formulated. This appears palpably, for example, during the long history of pedagogy, and in disputes concerning "education" from Rousseau onward. One passed from the hypothesis of men held to be equally good "according to nature," already possessing the possibility of behaving rightly if not manipulated and obliged from outside, to the contrary idea, according to which the variety of behavior was in any case inseparable from a people who were its bearers; this implied that there could be no hiatus between the individual and his ethnic customs. This was the case of the disputes raging over the native Aotourou's incapacity to learn "civilization," after his removal from Tahiti to Paris.

What escaped the consideration of such formulations was the fact that an individual psychological structure could exist in confrontation or conflict with a particular culture. But Boas had posed the problem in a different way. In stressing the phenomena of analogy and diffusion among given cultural traits, he had asked whether these had the same meaning for all peoples. Rituals, noted Boas, can pass from one people to another, but the significance that each people gives to the same series of gestures often varies; and thus it is necessary to discover what distinguishes one culture from another, by assuming the native point of view—not only from inside each single culture, but also on the basis of subjective experience. In a somewhat obscure way, a passage was now being made from the study of the global system, not to the individual one, but to an intermediate stage of a cultural psychology, of which all the individuals of the same group were held to be bearers.

Thus scholars began to attribute to each culture a "soul" or a "type," which colors, with its own particular hue, the set of customs of the people studied.

Ruth Benedict (1887–1948), a student of Boas, came to this very conclusion. She stated that culture, like the individual, is a more or less consistent pattern of thought and action. This pattern does not possess an ontological reality, and can therefore not be taken as a collective soul, but rather as a "style" of life, comparable to what is called "style" in the world of art (*Patterns of Culture*, 1934). At the same time, this style will be profoundly impressed on the individuals belonging to a given society, and will determine the varying aspects of their behavior.

At this point, then, psychology takes shape as one of anthropology's most difficult problems. The problem of the passage from individual to group psychology is, indeed, most complex and hard to pin down. Ruth Benedict says so explicitly in *Patterns of Culture*. Many modern sociologists and social psychologists, she points out, have tried to demonstrate with complicated arguments that society can never be anything different from or more than the individual minds composing it. Those who have studied other cultures have clearly realized that the laws of individual psychology are inadequate to explain the facts. The group, says Benedict, draws its force from tradition; it "withholds time." It can well be considered an organic whole. Such group phenomena, notes the scholar, must be studied if we wish to understand the history of human behavior; individual psychology is not sufficient to explain the facts we find ourselves confronting. The ingenuous interpretations of culture in terms of individual behavior are wrong, not because they are psychological interpretations, but because they fail to consider the history and historical process of the acceptance or refusal of certain elements. Any interpretation of culture aiming to define its configuration is expressed partly in terms of individual psychology, but is based on history no less than on psychology.

The problem, then, is that of the individual's integration into the culture of his group; one must ask to what degree one is psychologically molded by the group's culture. In other words, the question to ask is this: Is culture assumed by the individual as an external type of behavior that he accepts, or is it psychologically absorbed so deeply as to form the very structure of personality? In her approach, Ruth Benedict clearly touched on Boas's old problem: that of man's "biopsychic plasticity."

The same direction was taken by Margaret Mead, another student of Boas, though she was subject to various moments of hesitation and wavering during the course of her ethnological studies. From her research on Samoa and New Guinea, which became famous, Mead drew clear-cut conclusions. As a super-organism, as a set of relations, conventions and institutions, culture is only an abstraction of the spirit. Nothing exists but individuals, who construct or receive this culture, and who change it during the course of centuries. Man is the base, the foundation; it is to him we must look ("The Emergence of the Concept of Personality in the Study of Culture," 1934).

Thus the "personality culture" school was born in American anthropology: one particularly influenced by psychoanalysis. The anthropologists' acceptance of certain Freudian theories had the merit of introducing a dynamic dimension into the study of interpersonal relations. This was an extremely important contribution for ethnologists, nearly all of whom, given the very method used in their research, tended to possess a static vision of different cultures, and to set aside the problem of the relation between individual and culture. On the contrary, Freud stressed the importance of the child's earliest relations with his environment in his construction of the future, establishing a very close tie between society and the individual. Thus anthropologists began concentrating their attention on child-raising, nourishment, weaning, sexual education, and so on. This was the road followed by works such as Ruth Benedict's analysis of Japanese culture, *The Chrysanthemum and the Sword* (1946), and Gregory Bateson's and Mead's *Balinese Character* (1942).

In studying the connection between childhood and cultural manifestations, the latter emphasize the importance assumed in Balinese society by the mother's behavior, which is authoritarian and sexually stimulating (the mother sleeps lying on the son). It is the mother who regulates the children's conduct, and it is she who has the task of assuring that their marriage takes place within the clan. According to the authors, the attitude and power of the mother strongly mold the child's character, and so the Balinese adult's; certain Balinese traditions, certain dances and role-playing games can only be explained if we take into account the Balinese children's absolute dependence on their mothers.

Of course it would be possible here, as in many other cases, to reverse the initial hypothesis, since we can affirm that it is not the individual who models civilizations, but civilizations which model the individual. Indeed, in the case cited (as everywhere), mothers behave according to modes established by the cultural institutions in which they live, and not merely in function of their own emotional structure. This also touches on one of the most highly debated points of feminism today. In fact, mothers are accused of forming sons in such a way that they feel superior to the daughters, by inculcating aggressive values in them, exonerating them from household chores, and so on; they thus transmit a certain type of behavior from one generation to the next, creating a division between male and female roles which entails women's inferior condition. But it is clear that no mother "invents" any type of child education and upbringing, since these are rigid cultural institutions which the individual cannot avoid, and which are reflected and functionally interrelated in the area of the overall cultural pattern. It is also true that no one, not even the most independent woman, would know how to deal with the problem of a newborn baby unless environment and custom had predisposed actions capable of offering her security, and the certainty that she can do right by her child. For this is man's strength—this has allowed him to create culture: the capacity to find support in preceding experiences, handed down because society holds them to be useful; thus he is not obliged to "experiment" each gesture without having any notion of the result. If we are able to debate the problems linked to women's condition in our society today, therefore, it is only because we have begun to notice the existence of culture, and to discuss and doubt certain of its values. Only on the basis of this premise can the individual effort at non-acceptance and change start to become useful.

We are thus led back to Benedict's theory, which considers the different "types" of cultures, each with its own spirit and style. The theory of the "basic personality" formulated by Abram Kardiner attempted to resolve the problem by hypothesizing a common denominator in the personality of individuals belonging to the same group, and therefore to the same culture; a personality conditioned by the environment, which imposes its norms on the individual who, in turn, responds with a series of secondary psycho-emotional acts (*The Individual and His Society*, 1939). Kardiner's point of departure is Freudian, although he worked alongside an anthropologist, Ralph Linton, who furnished him with the ethnographic material for verifying his hypotheses.

Kardiner accepts Freud's premises, which consider civilization and culture both as a system of collective protection and as a solution to the problems posed by Oedipal conflicts inherent in childhood. In Kardiner's opinion, then, the individual's difficulties in adapting spring from the socio-cultural system itself, understood as a repressive agent—from the very beginning—in relation to instincts and aspirations. According to this viewpoint, on one hand, we shall have a constant, given by the individual's biological needs; on the other, we shall have variables, given by the institutions composing the various active external realities (the cultures).

In *The Individual and His Society*, Kardiner notes that environmental conditions, and some aspects of social organization included in the concept of primary institutions, create fundamental problems for the individuals' adaptation. An individual must develop certain methods for accepting demands which are fixed and immutable. The fundamental constellations created in the individual by these conditions, continues Kardiner, are the structure of his ego, subjectively considered; or if considered from an objective point of view, they are the structure of his basic personality.

The problem, then, is to discern the general aspects in the individual peculiarities of the character belonging to a given human group: generalities purportedly owing to cultural modeling. Indeed, Kardiner adds that the individual is obliged to react in a certain way; and whatever results as the form of the *individual character*, it is the institutional background that constitutes the axis around which the various "individual polarities" rotate.

Later on, Linton better defines this concept in a volume written in collaboration with Kardiner, *The Psychological Frontiers of Society* (1945). The *type of basic personality* in each society, he writes, is that configuration of personality which is shared by the majority of members in the society, resulting from the initial life experiences they have in common. It does not correspond to the individual's total personality, but to protective systems, or systems of attitudes toward values which are fundamental in the configuration of the individual's personality. Thus, continues Linton, the same type of basic personality can be reflected in many different types of behavior, and can pertain to many different configurations of the total personality.

Though it may seem contradictory, since it so explicitly stresses the importance of the environmental context, the hypothesis of the basic personality actually refers back to the biological problem, presupposing an instinctual endowment identical in all individuals, and so an equal "response" to equal cultural stimuli. The subjective, particular interaction with the cultural and historical data of one's existence, then, supposedly occurs only on the "basis" of a personality which is already formed. Moreover, this is a logical consequence of Kardiner's Freudian premises, which are of an instinctual character. The biological problem thus comes to the fore again, precisely when most emphasis is given to the force of culture in shaping personality. This problem appears in two perspectives.

On one hand, it is supposed that all individuals are biologically equal, even at a psychological level; on the other, a premise is eliminated which had been indispensable in Kroeber: i.e., that culture is an autonomous level of nature—one which can never be reabsorbed into the underlying levels included in it (*The Nature of Culture*, 1952).

At any rate, what distinctly emerges here is the immaturity and lack of clear theoretical formulations in both of the disciplines called upon—psychology and anthropology. The "basic personality" theory nonetheless ended up by assuming such formulations as certain, thus drastically diminishing the wealth of dramatic force in that concept of culture which scholars had fought so arduously to bring to light. Moreover, misunderstandings also arose from the lack of reflection (or better, acceptance) concerning the fundamental point of the culture concept: the accumulation and transformation due to the historical process.

Ruth Benedict notes as much in *Patterns of Culture*. The difficulty with all studies concerning social custom, she writes, lies in the fact that the behavior examined has had to pass through the filter of society, and only history in its vastest sense can explain that behavior's acceptances and refusals on the part of society. Not only psychology is involved here, she adds, but history as well; and history is certainly not a set of facts that can be explained through introspection.

The problem of the link between culture and personality was posed, discussed, resolved, and then debated anew by Margaret Mead in her famous research on male and female behavior in various cultures. It was taken for granted that differences in behavior between the male and female groups were most easily demonstrable as biological differences. In her preface to the 1950 edition of *Sex and Temperament in Three Primitive Societies* (the first had been published in 1935), Mead herself wrote, in 1931, that on going into the countryside, she had intended to study only one problem: the conditioning of personality in the two sexes. She hoped that such research might shed light on the *differences between the sexes*. But after two years of work, she notes, she realized that the material gathered shed light, instead, on *differences in temperament*: that is, on the *innate individual qualities*, independently of sex.

In fact, Margaret Mead came to the conclusion that cultures impose given values and forms of behavior on the basis of many artificial distinctions, "the most surprising of which is sex." In Mead's view, then, there are individual variations in the human temperament which can be equally present in the male and female, but which are either exalted or inculcated by the choices that cultures have made in the institutionalization of behavioral differences between the sexes.

Mead's theories underwent transformations and reconsideration during the long period of her field research. However, like Ruth Benedict, she continued to believe in the existence of a dialectic position of the individual temperament in relation to one's culture; in all cultures, she said, it is this position itself which gives rise to "aberrant" personalities, those unable to accept the roles and values imposed by society. One is thus led to ask whether mental illnesses objectively exist, and how they can be diagnosed, or whether they are only the result of the culture's imposition on personalities that cannot adapt to it. Meanwhile, the hypothesis of the existence of a basic personality as the psychological interjection of data and categories of one's culture gave rise to the theory of the "relativity of values" between different cultures. The major advocate of cultural relativism was Herskovits; but it was also proposed by Benedict, Mead, and Linton.

If we presuppose a departure potential which is different from one individual to the next, as affirmed in recent genetic theories (see Theodosius Dobzhansky, *Mankind Evolving*, 1962), then clearly a conflict can be unleashed between the individual and the culture. While such conflict can cause emotional unbalance and actual mental illness, it also allows us to explain cultural changes owing to the very interaction and conflict between culture and individuals. This perspective also allows us to clarify the difficult problem of the relativity of values, since in the course of the historical process, single individuals or groups are able to evaluate and confront different values, and so to make choices which, in the long run, will influence cultural transformation.

According to Herskovits's formula, the principle of cultural relativism can be summed up in the affirmation that judgments are based on experience, and experience is interpreted by each individual in terms of his own acculturation (*Man and His Works*,

1955). This claim is excessively drastic; it does not take into account the different situation in which each individual lives out his experiences in the interaction between his biological individuality and his cultural reality. In a society like the modern one, moreover, the possibilities of knowing other cultural choices besides one's own are quite different from what they were in the past. At any rate, it is worthwhile to consider philosopher David Bidney's observations as to Herskovits's invocation of respect for the values of all cultures. If cultural progress is a valid, objective ideal, he writes, the anthropologist, as one who studies culture and the dynamics of cultures compared with one another, must cooperate in the common task of indicating some of the conditions necessary for the achievement of progress, both in our cultures and in others. To insist on a cultural *laissez-faire* in the name of the madness and crimes of the ethnocentrism of the past is a desperate choice which fails to confront the real goals of humanity ("The Concept of Value in Modern Anthropology," 1953).

Of course, the crux of the problem lies in establishing whether and to what degree it is possible to form a framework for our judgments which is not defined a priori by our own traditional value system. True, the road traveled by Western culture has led to this possibility, for it is Western culture which allows itself self-analysis, and thus, self-doubt. If this doubt is a value, in the sense that it allows us to free ourselves of the "obviousness" of our own culture (which does not necessarily mean denying or rejecting it), then we certainly can also attempt to express judgments which, though based on this experience, may prove useful and valid. We find ourselves thrown here into a maelstrom of problems to which philosophers are more accustomed than anthropologists, even though, as Hans Gadamer observes, "anthropology is not only a problem *for* philosophy; it represents a problem *of* philosophy" (*Le problème de la conscience historique*, 1963).

Yet no one more than the anthropologist finds himself facing the need to solve the problem of values in some way: to express judgments on cultures in a world like today's, in which acculturating exchanges become even more traumatic that those of the old colonialism. Suffice it to consider the turmoil of so many countries in the so-called Third World, in which Western technology and political ideas attempt to coexist with cultural traits belonging to the old patterns, thus lacerating what constitutes the strength of every culture: the functional, meaningful interconnection of all its traits and values. At any rate, the most emblematic case is our own, that of Western culture. For it is here, and here alone that, as Gadamer says, the most important revolution has occurred: the emergence of an historical conscience. He writes:

> By "historical awareness" we mean modern man's privilege to have full awareness of the historicity of every present and the relativity of opinions... From now on it would be absurd to confine oneself in the naiveté and reassuring limits of an exclusive tradition, when modern awareness is prepared to understand the possibility of a multiplicity of relative viewpoints.... To have a sense of history means thinking expressly of the historical horizon which is coextensive with the life that we are living and have lived [*Le problème de la conscience historique*].

But if it is a privilege, this "coextension" is also an enormous burden, under which we are always about to succumb, given the duality that has been created between our awareness, which tends to break through the cultural encirclement, and the "need" (in Malinowski's sense) to reconstitute each day the meaningful unity of our cultural existence. This situation increases our psychic distress, for the lack of a strong, coherent cultural model becomes a source of insecurity for psychologically fragile personalities who cannot find a structure to cling to, and a source of conflict for psychologically strong personalities who are unable to tolerate the burden of incoherence.

For the first time, then, the problem of anthropology's relation to psychiatry emerges. So does the problem of ethnopsychiatric comparison.

The Problem of Psychiatry and Transcultural Psychiatry

In the fluid situation characterizing psychiatry today, which is profoundly influenced by anthropological discoveries and the relativity of cultural values, we must be very cautious in approaching the problem of the relationship between anthropology and psychiatry, all the more so in that we lack precise statistical data and detailed clinical monographs. The first ethnologists who turned their attention to mental disturbances in societies different from ours were particularly struck by the most dramatic cases, such as arctic hysteria, latah, amok, and windigo psychosis. This attitude gave rise to a restricted, even false image of pathological forms of behavior in the populaces studied. In other cases, there was a tendency to judge certain phenomena which were frequent in given cultures, such as "possession," as unquestionably abnormal, merely because in our culture they are so considered.

A long, arduous period thus had to pass before transcultural psychiatric research could take its first steps. Paradoxically, as progress was made in this direction, the definition of illness and normality became more and more challenging in any cultural context, including our own.

Moreover, in whatever environment they operate, psychiatrists (especially those with an exclusively medical background) tend to apply the habitual diagnostic classifications. This further complicates the situation, since gaps in statistical data and an insufficient analysis of various cases are aggravated by the contradictions and different interpretations of the psychiatric schools themselves.

According to some authors, for example, no schizophrenics are found in Africa (except among "Westernized" populaces), nor are there any paranoids; while other scholars, instead, claim that schizophrenia, at least in its atypical forms, is not rare in traditional societies, and that if paranoia seems absent, that is because it is somehow covered up and dissimulated by religious rituals. However, all such information began to appear in a methodically organized form only a short time ago, partly because the question of schizophrenia as an illness of "civilization" undoubtedly entailed many emotional factors and value judgments regarding the culture to which the scholars themselves belonged.

It was not until 1961, at the third World Congress of Psychiatry, that the first systematic study on the frequency of schizophrenia in non–Western countries was made public. On that occasion, scholars also affirmed the importance of socio-cultural values in the development of mental illness, as well defining the symptoms that may appear in delirium in individuals belonging to a given culture. During the same congress, Ruth Benedict's fundamental concept was proposed once more: The norm is to be judged in relation to the cultural pattern that has molded the individual.

Transcultural psychiatric research officially began in 1954, with J.C.D. Carothers' study on "Mental Health and Illness in the African," commissioned by the World Health Organization. But the steps that followed were slow. In 1957, the psychiatrist Erich D. Wittkower established a Department of Transcultural Psychiatry at McGill University in Montreal, and the periodical *Transcultural Psychiatric Research* was founded with the intention of spreading the anthropological-psychiatric studies carried out in different cultural areas. In 1964, at the World Congress of Social Psychiatry, a section was dedicated to transcultural psychiatry; finally, in 1965, the Society of African Psychopathology was founded in Dakar by the psychiatrist Henri Collomb, who also directed the review, *Psychopathologie Africaine*.

The main problem here was to clarify whether differences in judgment between anthropologists and psychiatrists sprang merely from contradictions and diagnostic errors, or whether their methods were diametrically opposed. Edward Sapir pointed out this contrast between the two disciplines starting with their earliest attempts at collaboration, stressing the intimate interaction between society as a psychological and cultural unity, and the individual as a member of the society, from which he draws all the elements necessary for orienting himself in the world and for placing his ego in relation to reality (*Cultural Anthropology and Psychiatry*, 1932). Cultural anthropology, in fact, does not start by considering individual variations, it annuls them, whereas psychiatry is exclusively concerned with deviations in individual behavior. The psychiatrist, indeed, starts out from individual cases in order to arrive at culture, while the anthropologist starts out from social norms, institutions, and myths, in order to reach an understanding of individual behavior, including pathological behavior. This methodological difference creates a situation in which the respective research conclusions not only fail to complement one another, but even contradict one another. In fact, if culture is perceived as something external to individuals, and somehow "added on" to the personality from outside, then mental illnesses are explained according to the conflict between society and individual. On the other hand, if culture is held to be an abstraction, and the existence of norms is totally internalized, then these illnesses will be attributed to the conflict between contradictory values within the individual. Or else, according to Benedict's hypothesis, they will be attributed to the discontinuity of roles, as occurs in Western society.

Naturally, as noted before, the first problem facing us in the field of ethnopsychiatry is to define what is "normal" and what is "pathological." With this aim, scholars have proposed several fundamental criteria of a psychiatric, statistic, and cultural nature. The cultural criterion, formerly proposed by Ruth Benedict, states that forms of behavior considered as abnormal in our culture are not considered so in different cultures ("Mental Illness in Primitive Societies," 1954). In other words, madness is just as relative as mental health, so unless the psychiatrist detaches himself from the values of his own culture, he cannot formulate any diagnosis that is not a value judgment as well.

According to Benedict, just as those whose natural reactions are nearest the behavior characterizing their society are privileged, so those whose reactions fall within the behavior range rejected by their culture are disoriented. These abnormal persons cannot find confirmation for their inclinations in the institutions of their civilization; they are the exceptions—those unable to accept the traditional forms of the society in which they were born. For comparative psychiatry, it is extremely important to study such individuals. All too often in psychiatry, problems have been complicated by starting from a fixed list of symptoms, instead of studying persons whose characteristic reactions are rejected by the society in which they live (*Patterns of Culture*).

Benedict then calls attention to another highly important point, noting that psychiatrists do not concern themselves with those "abnormal" persons who, instead, represent the extreme development of the local ideal type. From a social point of view, in fact, this group's situation is the opposite from that of the non-integrated group. Instead of abandoning them, society sustains these "abnormal" persons in their most extreme aberrations, granting them limitless freedom and prestige, as occurs in the case of religious and political leaders. Therefore, these individuals are hardly ever the objects of inquiry for the psychiatrists of their time;

but they may be judged as psychopaths by a later generation, or by a different culture. (This touches on such highly discussed pathological personalities as Hitler's.)

Of course, in a position of this kind one risks confusing "deviance" as a purely sociological abnormality with true mental illness—one having an organic cause as well. That is why Clyde Kluckhohn, an anthropologist profoundly interested in the relation between personality and culture, entered into the debate, insisting that all cultures must necessarily consider as abnormal those individuals whose behavior cannot be foreseen according to the cultural norms, with whom one can never communicate, or who are incapable of controlling their instincts ("The Influence of Psychiatry on Anthropology in America," 1944). Ralph Linton follows the same line in distinguishing absolute abnormality from relative abnormality. Absolute abnormality is held to have an organic cause; the individual is incapable of experiencing reality according to the way it is perceived by his society. Relative abnormality, instead, consists of the individual's poor adaptation to his cultural environment: poor adaptation which creates an excessive distance between his personality and the basic personality (*Culture and Mental Disorders*, 1956).

Georges Devereux, instead, claims that a psychiatric abnormality can exist in individuals even when cultures exploit that abnormality, as in the case of shamans or sorcerers. Not only does he distinguish between normal and ill individuals, but also between normal societies and ill ones (*Essais d'ethnopsychiatrie générale*, 1970). The supposed utility of the shaman for the tribe to which he belongs, says Devereux, does not in the least prove that he is normal. It only proves the disorder of the entire tribe, whose latent conflicts the shaman reflects to the extreme. In certain respects, this position approaches the one assumed by Ruth Benedict in defining the Kwakiutl culture as paranoid, thus using our psychiatric categories to explain patterns different from our own; except that Benedict, unlike Devereux, did not intend to explicitly attribute a pathological valence to the cultures she describes. Benedict went back to reconsider the problem, accepting the principle of a "relative abnormality" (on the basis of which, as she had previously stated in *Patterns of Culture*, individuals who are normal in one culture may be abnormal in another); and of an "absolute abnormality," definable according to a fixed set of symptoms, treatable by psychiatrists (*Anthropology and the Abnormal*, 1934).

The problem had already been anticipated by Freud, when he observed that the institutionalized mode of prohibition by taboo in primitive societies evokes, in its rigidity, the mode found in the obsessive neurotic. However, at the time, Freud's bold analogies were severely contested by ethnologists. After all, how can one demonstrate that the system of tabooing is only a mode of collective obsession which avoids pathological mechanisms precisely because it is institutionalized? The question of whether or not pathological societies exist or whether, instead, there are individuals within single cultures who experience their neurosis in a normal manner because it is absorbed by institutions is one of the most difficult ones to answer, both for the anthropologist and for the psychiatrist. It touches on the very possibility of defining mental illness.

In the attempt to establish the existence of mental illness, then, another criterion was proposed: the statistical one. Similar to the cultural criterion, it nonetheless tends to eliminate, as far as possible, any residue of ethnocentrism. If reactions which seem pathological to us are commanded by norms (as, for example, among the Kwakiutl), we would have to admit that we find ourselves facing normal cultural mechanisms; abnormal behavior would only be that which not only deviates from general behavior, but is considered abnormal by the majority of individuals belonging to the same society. But here, aside from the criticism previously made on the basis of theories distinguishing a cultural abnormality from a natural or absolute abnormality, we must note that the statistics refer only to observable forms of behavior, and not to the causes of behavior; whereas it is the causes themselves which define a natural abnormality. Therefore we should keep social maladjustment separate from maladjustment caused by mental disturbance.

Anthropology and psychiatry could collaborate only after clearly defining their respective fields of inquiry. Of course, it is also difficult for the psychiatrist to judge phenomena which in different areas in our society appear as pathological: for example, those involving "possession" by spirits, which are widespread in various cultures; or the presence of hallucinations among the Plains Indians during initiation (see Ruth Benedict, "The Vision in Plains

Culture," 1922). Indeed, such phenomena can be considered conditioned reflexes, created by society and aiming to achieve goals useful for the community; after all, the "possessed" person is not abandoned to his inner world, but performs the exact role that his culture's mythology attributes to the divinity possessing him. Even in cases where the trance takes on a more spectacular character, reaching violent manifestations apparently similar to those of hysteria, the "possessed" person always remains under the control of and in communication with those assisting him, and the violence of his crises serves to manifest the violence of the possessing god or spirit, thus revealing itself as a logical form of compliance with the mythological model.

Apropos of "possession," separate mention should be made as regards "mental illness" in women. A fairly emblematic case is found in an exclusively female cult, Bori, practiced by the African ethnic group of the Hausa. Once she has fallen ill out of vengeance by the gods, against whom she has sinned, the woman—and future priestess—can be saved and healed only through repentance and adhesion to the Bori cult. Bori, like so many other cults of possession, is cathartic. Having been cured physically and psychologically, the disciple finds an outlet for a difficult, ambiguous personality, within the positive, prestigious role of "receptacle of the gods." She becomes a healer, whom the society surrounding her appreciates more than any other person. The position of the woman as the "gods' mare" in Hausa Bori is emblematic, and extraordinarily explicative of all the ambiguities with which the woman performs her role in relation to society, culture, religion, and "power." In order to achieve "male" power (which among the Hausa is that of the healer), the woman must pass through a metamorphosis which transforms her from a guilty person into one "chosen by the gods"; from one "useless" because ill or sterile, into an "instrument" functional to society. Mediation with the sacred is, at any rate, a guarantee against any risk: The woman's power belongs to her only in secondary form; it is a "delegated" power, hardly capable of exalting or defining her, since it depends exclusively on the will of the gods.

The problem of mental illness in women in relation to their special position in various societies and cultures has not yet been truly confronted. But doubtlessly, women, much more so than men, are forced to seek refuge in a spectacular kind of mental illness which, in confirming the functions assigned to them as instruments for communication with the transcendent, can induce the group to reintegrate them into a social role.

The psychiatric judgment given on an ethnological level is therefore hard to apply; yet psychiatrists and anthropologists today no longer nourish any doubt as to the existence of hysterical individuals, psychopaths, and neurotics in any part of the world, recognized and treated as such, though in a different manner from ours. At the second Pan-African Conference on Psychiatry (1968), the general tendency of the scholars was thus to simultaneously recognize the fundamental unity of the great psychopathological processes, and the diversity of their external manifestations, which are tied to social and cultural factors. Laubscher's study of a Bantu ethnic group, for example, finds that cultural differences do not influence the structure of the psychotic reactions to the point of making it different from the one present in Western society, even though the cultural pattern to which the subject belongs determines the nature of his mental behavior (*Sex, Custom, and Psychopathology*, 1937).

The role played by cultural factors in psychiatric symptoms and contents is particularly evident in patients suffering from delirium—from ideas of persecution and possession, which are modeled on beliefs in the supernatural. Among the Wolof, one of the most important ethnic groups of Senegal, people strongly believe in the intervention of ancestral spirits and evil spirits; and in the evil action of sorcerers, the most dangerous of whom is the "man-eating sorcerer," who tries to deprive a man of his vital spirit. These different beliefs are first reflected in the fears or delirious ideas of ill people, and then in the therapeutical methods applied—often successfully—by different types of traditional healers. Thus the same belief can exercise a pathogenic effect on the individual and, at the same time, serve as a vehicle for the healer's therapeutic action. (Systematic studies of traditional native psychotherapies were carried out for several years in the University Clinic of Dakar, formerly directed by Henri Collomb.)

Furthermore, the primitives make a distinction between mental disturbances and collective magic or religious manifestations, although the causes they give may be very different from causes as

Westerners see them. At any rate, it is important for the ethnologist, as well as for the psychiatrist, to know whether mental illnesses are rarer among the "primitives" than among us, and to what degree they may be due to constitutional factors, poor nourishment, customs, and other causes. According to Laubscher, for example, the preference for marriages between first or second cousins explains the high percentage of typical hereditary mental diseases in certain primitive societies (*Sex, Custom, and Psychopathology*). When all is said and done, however, pathological personalities, like normal ones, cannot be detached from the context of interpersonal relations, the collective realities in which they live, or the cultural experiences they undergo. Mental disorders are thus to be considered as total responses of personality to various, well-defined social contexts, and to an entire set of collective values (Morris Edward Opler, *Culture and Mental Health*, 1959).

Georges Devereux: Normality and Abnormality in Cultures

In the personality-culture school, psychoanalysis very heavily influenced anthropology, whereas, vice versa, anthropology had influenced psychoanalysis for many years previously, starting with the Freudian analogy between the primitive, the child and the neurotic. A basic question remains, in any case: Is there a difference of a biological nature between different individuals' responses to cultural stimuli, implying the existence of an absolute abnormality, or is the normal/abnormal concept always relatable to single cultural contexts? Furthermore, according to what criteria, and on the basis of what symptoms, can the concept of normality/abnormality be fixed?

As is well-known, according to Freud, cultural variants are not significant in themselves, since they are considered exclusively evolutionary stages of an identical collective psyche within the history of all mankind. One of Freud's disciples, however, Geza Roheim, took up a distinct position. He did not support the hypothesis of a relationship between culture and the drama of the origins of the primitive horde which, in Freud's view, was supposed to have left an indelible mark on the inherited memory of all men. Instead,

Roheim attributes the main role in the constitution of various cultural patterns and institutions to the extraordinary duration of human infancy, and to the tensions connected with it because of the child's necessary dependence on the mother and, therefore, its difficulty in acquiring an autonomous ego. Still, Roheim fundamentally moves within the psychoanalytical context when, for example, he claims the analogy between the technique of dream analysis and that of cultural analysis. In *Psychoanalysis and Anthropology* (1950), he notes that if we isolated each element of dreams from its context, we would never succeed in discovering the unconscious content. The manifest expression of the dream, he adds, only corresponds to what the dream seems to be, and the same can be said of culture.

To Roheim, we owe the fundamental intuition that elements repressed in one culture often remain in an unconscious state in another. This intuition was to become a true theoretical hypothesis in Georges Devereux, Roheim's student. Devereux adopts psychoanalysis in two ways: on one hand, in order to delineate a scientific concept of culture, and on the other, in maintaining that, from the epistemological point of view, the processes of transference and countertransference brought to light by psychoanalytical therapy are also verified in the anthropological study of cultures.

One Freudian theory which Devereux accepts in full is that of the unity of the human psyche: "the human mind functions in a nearly identical way everywhere, especially in situations of stress, when under the effect of tension, the 'old Adam' reappears, more or less in his primitive nudity, stripped of the supports and chains of culture" (*Ethnopsychanalyse complémentariste*, 1972).

Devereux, however, does not intend to take the psychic unity of man in a rigid sense; in fact, it includes the concept of an extreme capacity for variation, which is actualized by culture itself. Psychic unity subsists, instead, particularly in the sphere of the unconscious. That is why, according to Devereux, primitive men, in whom human potential has not been completely actualized and in whom the unconscious dimension dominates, are very similar to one another, as are neurotics and persons in a state of stress, in whom a phenomenon of "deculturation" takes place. A neurotic Cheyenne Indian and a neurotic Maori, who are necessarily psychotic, resemble a neurotic and psychotic American more than normal Cheyennes or Maoris resemble normal Americans, he notes (*Cultural Factors in Psychoanalytic Therapy*, 1953). According to Devereux, then, there is a strict correlation between the uniformity of the individual psyche and the uniformity of human culture; in fact, it is possible to affirm that if all psychoanalysts compiled a list of all the instincts, all the desires, and all the phantoms brought to light clinically, these would correspond point by point to an analogous list of all the beliefs and cultural processes we know of, defined by ethnologists (*A Study of Abortion in Primitive Societies*, 1955). Moreover, Devereux states that, like the psyche, the culture which reflects it is uniform in its constitutive elements; that is why traits repressed in one society can become conscious and attain cultural expression in another. "The uniformity of the human psyche also implies the uniformity of human culture, with a capital 'C'. Like individuals, cultures differ essentially in the way in which their constitutive elements are juxtaposed and organized into patterns and structures" (*Essais d'ethnopsychiatrie générale*).

Cultures also differ from each other in that a given item can have as a primary matrix in one culture what actually constitutes its latent content in another: "In fact, I consider that the systematic affirmation of a belief necessarily implies a negation of the opposite belief, and that this negation is just as much an integral part of the culture ... as the affirmation itself. Thus, for example, Islam's categorical affirmation of absolute monotheism proves the latent, repressed existence of polytheistic ideas" (*Essais d'ethnopsychiatrie générale*). As regards the problem of the basic personality, Devereux refers exclusively to the formation of the unconscious, which he subdivides into two parts. The ethnic unconscious is that part of the individual's total unconscious that he possesses in common with most of the members of his culture; it is composed of everything which, in conformity with the needs of the culture, each generation learns to repress, forcing the succeeding generation to do the same. On the basis of the existence of the ethnic unconscious, one can suppose that all the members of the same culture suffer from a certain number of similar inner conflicts. The "idiosyncratic" unconscious, instead, is that part of the individual unconscious which is formed on the basis of "private" stress, belonging exclusively to personal experience.

At any rate, what interests us most in Devereux's theories from an anthropological point of view is the hypothesis regarding those psychic disturbances that he calls "sacred," which are supposedly localized in the ethnic unconscious. From an interdisciplinary perspective, this hypothesis directly touches on the very concept of culture, especially as regards the individual's adaptation to his culture when the culture itself is "ill." In other words, Devereux does not identify the institutionalization of a role with the adaptation to the culture by the individual assuming the role itself. Two quite convincing examples, reported by Devereux, refer to homosexuality among the Mohave Indians in California, among whom he lived for a lengthy period, and to shamanism, as experienced among various Siberian populaces. Among the Mohave, (male) sexuality is a frequent, highly institutionalized practice. Mohave culture, then, provides a means of expression for the homosexual drives in some of its members, officially recognizing a form of personality deviation which is in contrast with the group's ethnic ideal (*Institutionalized Homosexuality of the Mohave Indians*, 1937). However, the homosexual, even while having a culturally typical, explicit role, is not for that reason a "normal" element of the group to which he belongs. His drives remain out of tune with his culture, precisely because the conflict is situated in his ethnic unconscious; and the Mohave crowd witnessing the most scabrous manifestations of the homosexual, ridiculing and inciting them, thus tries to appease the ethnic conflicts of the unconscious.

In Devereux's view, the situation of the shaman is similar. Though he is a seriously neurotic or psychotic individual in a state of temporary remission, his conflicts are localized in the ethnic unconscious of the group to which he belongs. But precisely because the shaman's conflicts engage the ethnic segment of his personality, they are similar to those of the "normal" members of his tribe. This explains why they participate in his "ritualized" symptoms, finding reassurance against their anxiety. Arguing against the cultural relativists, then, Devereux maintains that the shaman is not "normal" for the fact that his beliefs are common to all the members of his culture, but on the contrary, that the institution of shamanism proves the presence of latent conflicts in the ethnic unconscious of the group, which—precisely for that reason—finds a calming, cathartic effect in the symptoms ritualized by the shaman (*Essais d'ethnopsychiatrie générale*).

If this is true, then when are a culture and society more or less healthy? According to Devereux, a culture is "healthy" when it favors the most complete actualization and, at the same time, individualization of all its members. They must be able to establish a continual dialectic relationship with their culture, as "creators, creatures, manipulators and transmitters" of the culture itself.

In concluding this brief survey of problems involved in the relation between psychology, psychoanalysis and anthropology, and while admitting that vast uncertainties remain, we cannot help but stress the wealth of data, implications and hypotheses which anthropology, with its concept of culture, has brought, not only to psychology, but to all the human sciences.

The path lying ahead is long and arduous. It is a path to be traveled using the comparative method, by recognizing the differences and similarities among the various human groups, not as an instrument for deciding, once and for all, which choices are best, but only as a means for framing the old questions on a vaster horizon.

With anthropology, questions which were once delegated to philosophy alone now emerge at their root level.

Does today's awareness of the existence of an unconscious sphere not influence the mechanisms of the unconscious itself? Does the knowledge of the relativity of our perception of space and time not influence our very way of experiencing space and time? Does an awareness of the cultural pressures on the structure of the individual personality not influence the very constitution of personality?

Once again, the problem becomes that of humanity's "historicity," and the burden of historical awareness on its future. Anthropology emerges simply as a method capable of widening human historical awareness, synchronically and diachronically, to the furthest possible frontiers.

Bibliography

Acosta, S. de. *Historia general y moral de las Indias.* Mexico and Buenos Aires: Fondo de Cultura Economica, 1962.
Adkins, A.W.H. *Moral Values and Political Behaviour in Ancient Greece.* London: Chatto and Windus, 1972.
Amat, P. *Biografia dei viaggiatori italiani e bibliografia delle loro opere.* Rome: Tipografia Elzeviriana, 1875.
Bachelard, G. *Epistémologie: Textes choisis.* Paris: Presses Universitaires de France, 1971.
Bachofen, J.J. *Das Mutterecht.* Basel: Schwabe, 1897.
Baillie, J. *Belief in Progress.* Oxford: Oxford University Press, 1950.
Bastian, A. *Der Mensch in der Geschichte.* Leipzig: O. Wigand, 1860.
Bateson, G., and Mead, M. *Balinese Character.* New York: Academy of Sciences, 1942.
Bateson, S. *Naven.* Stanford: Leland Stanford Junior University, 1958 (1931).
Benedict, R. *Anthropology and the Abnormal.* N.p., 1934.
_____. *The Chrysanthemum and the Sword.* Boston: Houghton Mifflin, 1946.
_____. *Patterns of Culture.* New York: Houghton Mifflin, 1959 (1934).
_____. "The Vision in Plains Culture," *American Anthropologist,* XXIV, 1922.
_____, and Irvings, J. "Mental Illness in Primitive Societies," *Psychiatry,* XVII, 1954.
Benveniste, E. *Le vocabulaire des institutions indo-européenes.* Paris: Éditions de Minuit, 1969.
Bidney, D., ed. *The Concept of Freedom in Anthropology.* Paris and The Hague: Mouton, 1963.
_____. "The Concept of Value in Modern Anthropology," in A.L. Kroeber, ed., *Anthropology Today: An Encyclopedic Inventory.* Chicago: University of Chicago Press, 1959 (c.1953).
Boas, F., ed. *General Anthropology.* New York: Heath, 1938.
_____. "The Limitations of the Comparative Method of Anthropology

(1896)," *Race, Language and Culture.* New York: Macmillan, 1948.

———. *The Mind of Primitive Man,* in Thomas, W. (ed.), *Source Book for Social Origins.* Chicago: University of Chicago Press, 1911, pp. 143–155.

———. "Recent Anthropology," *Science,* XCVIII, 1943.

———. "Religion," in *Handbook of American Indian Languages: Linguistic Families of America North of Mexico.* Lincoln: University of Nebraska Press, 1966.

———. "Rudolph Virchow's Anthropological Work," *Science,* XVI, 1902.

Calame-Griaule, Geneviève. *Ethnologie et langage: La parole chez les Dogons.* Paris: Gallimard, 1965.

Cardona, G. *Introduzione all'etnolinguistica.* Bologna: Il Mulino, 1976.

Charlevoix, F.X. de. *Histoire et description générale de la Nouvelle France.* Paris, 1744.

Chinard, G. *L'Amérique et le reve exotique dans la littérature française au XVIIe et XVIIIe siècle.* Paris: Hachette, 1934.

Codrington, R.H. *The Melanesians: Studies in Their Anthropology and Folklore.* Oxford: Clarendon Press, 1891.

Condorcet, Marquis de, M.S.A. *Esquisse d'un tableau historique des progrès de l'esprit humain.* Paris: Masson, 1822 (1785).

Crosby, A.W. *The Columbian Exchange: Biological and Cultural Consequences of 1492.* Westport, Conn.: Greenwood Press, 1972.

Démeunier, J.N. *L'Esprit des usages et des coutumes des différents peuples.* London and Paris: Pissot, 1776.

Devereux, G. *Abortion in America.* H. Rosen, ed., pp. 95–152. Boston: Beacon Press, 1967.

———. *Essais d'ethnopsychiatrie générale.* Paris: Gallimard, 1973 (2nd ed.).

———. *Ethnopsychanalyse complémentariste* (*Ethnopsychoanalysis: Psychoanalysis and Anthropology as Complementary Frames of Reference*). Berkeley: University of California Press, 1978 (1972).

———. *A Study of Abortion in Primitive Societies.* New York: Julian Press, 1955.

Di Nola, A. "Potenza," *Enciclopedia delle religioni.* Florence: Vallecchi, IV, cc. 1744–1765.

Dobzhansky, T. *Mankind Evolving.* New Haven, Conn.: Yale University Press, 1962.

Dodds, E.R. *The Ancient Concept of Progress and Other Essays.* Oxford: Clarendon Press, 1973.

———. *Pagan and Christian in an Age of Anxiety.* Cambridge: Cambridge University Press, 1965.

Duchet, M. *Anthropologie et Histoire au siècle des lumières.* Paris: Masperot, 1971.

Dumézil, G. *The Destiny of the Warrior.* Chicago: University of Chicago Press, 1970.

Durkheim, E. *Les formes élémentaires de la vie religieuse.* Paris: F. Alcan, 1912.
Edelman, G. *Bright Air, Brilliant Fire.* New York: Basic Books, Inc., 1992.
———. *The Remembered Present.* New York: Basic Books, Inc., 1989.
Ehrenreich, P. *Die allgemeine Mythologie und ihre ethnologischen Grundlagen.* Berlin, 1910.
Eliade, M. *Myths, Dreams and Mysteries.* Trans. P. Mairet. New York: Harper & Row, 1960 (1957).
———, and Kitagawa, J.M. (ed.). *The History of Religions: Essays in Methodology.* Chicago: University of Chicago Press, 1959.
Elliott, S. *First Images of America: The Impact of the New World on the Old.* Cambridge: Cambridge University Press, 1970.
Emeneau, M.B. "Franz Boas as a Linguist," in Kroeber, A.L. et al. *Franz Boas 1858–1942.* Menasha, Wisc.: American Anthropological Association, 1943.
Engels, F. *Der Ursprung der Familie, des Privateigentums und des Staats.* 1884. English trans. *The Origin of the Family, Private Property, and the State.* New York: International Publishers, 1972.
Evans-Pritchard, E.E. *Theories of Primitive Religion.* London: Oxford University Press, 1959.
Fantini, B. *L'Evoluzionismo.* N.p., 1976.
Ferrand, G. *Relations de voyages et textes géographiques arabes, persans et turks relatifs à l'Extreme-Orient du VIIIe au XVIII siècles, traduits, revus et annotés.* Paris: E. Leroux, 1913.
Finley, M.J. *Economy and Society in Ancient Greece.* London: Chatto and Windus, 1981.
Firth, R., ed. *Man and Culture: An Evaluation of the Work of Bronislaw Malinowski.* London: Routledge and Kegan Paul, 1957.
Formigari, L. *Linguistica e antropologia nel secondo Settecento.* Messina: La Libra, 1972.
Frazer, J. "Taboo and the Perils of the Soul," *The Golden Bough.* London: Macmillan, 1911–1915 (1890).
Freud, S. *Civilization and Its Discontents.* Trans. J. Rivière. London: Hogarth, 1957.
———. *Totem and Taboo.* Trans. J. Strachey. New York: Norton, 1950.
Friedlander, S. *Histoire et Psychanalyse.* Paris: Editions du Seuil, 1975.
Gadamer, H.G. *Il problema della conscienza storica.* Naples: Guida, 1969 (1963).
Geertz, C. *Works and Lives: The Anthropologist as Author.* Stanford: Stanford University Press, 1988.
Gilli, G.A. *Origini dell'eguaglianza.* Turin: Einaudi, 1988.
Giraud-Teulon, A., *Les Origines dela Famille.* Genève, 1874.
Gliozzi, G. *La scoperta dei selvaggi: Antropologia e colonialismo da Colombo a Diderot.* Messina: Principato, 1971.
Goody, S., ed. *Literacy in Traditional Societies.* Cambridge: Cambridge University Press, 1968.

Greene, J.C. *The Death of Adam.* Ames: Iowa State University Press, 1959.
Gusdorf, G. *Introduction aux sciences humaines.* Paris: Les Belles Lettres, 1960.
Haddon, A.C. *A History of Anthropology.* London: Watts, 1910.
Hahn, E. *Das Alter der wirtschaftlichen Kultur der Menschheit.* Heidelberg: Winter, 1905.
Hall, E.T. *The Hidden Dimension.* New York: Doubleday, 1959.
_____. *The Silent Language.* Garden City, N.Y.: Doubleday, 1966.
Harris, M. *The Rise of Anthropological Theory: A History of Theories of Culture.* New York: Crowell, 1969 (2nd ed.).
Hartmann, H. "Psychoanalysis and Sociology," in S. Lorand, ed., *Psychoanalysis Today.* New York: International University Press, 1944.
Hazard, P. *La crisi della coscienza europea.* Milan: Il Saggiatore, 1968.
Herskovits, M.J. *Franz Boas: The Science of Man in the Making.* New York and London: Scribners, 1953.
_____. *Man and His Works.* New York: Knopf, 1955 (c.1948).
Hertz, R.K. *Death and the Right Hand.* Glencoe, Ill.: Free Press, 1960 (1909).
Hervé, G. "Montesquieu. L'ethnographie dans l'Esprit des Lois: la théorie des climats," *Revue de l'Ecole d'Anthropologie de Paris,* XVII, 1907, pp. 337–353.
Hodgen, M.T. *Early Anthropology in the 16th and 17th Centuries.* Philadelphia: University of Pennsylvania Press, 1964.
Hoebel, E.A. *The Law of Primitive Man.* Cambridge, Mass.: Harvard University Press, 1967.
_____. *Man in the Primitive World.* New York: McGraw-Hill, 1949.
Horton, R., and Finnegan, R. *Modes of Thought: Essays on Thinking in Western and Non-Western Societies.* London: Faber and Faber, 1973.
Hubert, R. *Les sciences sociales dans l'Encyclopédie.* Paris: Alcan, 1923.
Hume, D. *The Natural History of Religion.* Stanford: Stanford University Press, 1979.
Hymes, D.H., ed. *Language in Culture and Society: A Reader in Linguistics and Anthropology.* New York: Harper & Row, 1964.
_____. "Notes Toward a History of Linguistic Anthropology," *Anthropological Linguistics,* V, 1963, pp. 59–63.
Jakobson, R. "Franz Boas' Approach to Language," *International Journal of American Linguistics,* X, 1944, pp. 188–197.
Jensen. A.E. *Das religiose Weltbild einer fruhen Kultur.* Stuttgart: August Schroder Verlag, 1948.
Jésuites, Rélations des. 6 vol. Montréal: Éditions du Jour, 1972.
Jones, E. "The Psychology of Religion," in S. Lorand, ed., *Psychoanalysis Today.* New York: International University Press, 1944.
Jousse, M. *L'anthropologie du geste.* Paris: Gallimard, 1974.
Jung, C.G. *Psychology of the Unconscious: A Study of the Transforma-*

tions and Symbolisms of the Libido. New York: Dodd & Mead, 1957 (c.1916).

Jurieu, P. *Histoire critique des dogmes et des cultes bons et mauvais qui ont été dans l'Eglise depuis Adam jusqu'à Jésus-Christ.* Amsterdam: Chez François L'Honoré, 1704.

Kaberry, P.M. *Aboriginal Woman: Sacred and Profane.* Philadelphia: Blakiston Company, 1939.

Kardiner, A., ed. *The Individual and His Society.* New York: Columbia University Press, 1939.

Klemm, G.E. *Allgemeine Kulturgeschichte der Menschheit.* Leipzig: Teubner, 1843–1852.

Kluckhohn, C. "The Influence of Psychiatry on Anthropology in America," in J.K. Hall, ed., *One Hundred Years of American Psychiatry.* New York: Columbia University Press, 1944.

_____, and Murray, H.A. *Personality in Nature, Society and Culture.* New York: Knopf, 1948.

Kroeber, A.L. *Anthropology: Race, Language, Culture, Psychology, Prehistory.* New York: Harcourt, Brace & World, 1948 (1923).

_____. *Configurations of Culture Growth.* Berkeley: University of California Press, 1944.

_____. *Cultural and Natural Areas of Native North America.* Berkeley: University of California Press, 1939.

_____. "The Eighteen Professions," *American Anthropologist,* XXVII, 1915, pp. 283–289.

_____. "History and Science in Anthropology," *American Anthropologist,* XXXVII, 1935, pp. 539–569.

_____. *The Nature of Culture.* Chicago: University of Chicago Press, 1952.

_____, ed. *Anthropology Today.* Chicago and London: University of Chicago Press, 1959 (6th ed.).

_____, and Kluckhohn, C. *Culture: A Critical Review of Concepts and Definitions.* New York: Vintage Books, 1963.

Lafiteau, J.T. *Moeurs des Sauvages Amériquains comparées aux moeurs des premiers temps.* Paris: Saugrain L'Ainé, 1721.

Lang, A. *The Making of Religion.* London: Longmans, Green, 1898.

Langendoen, D.T. *The London School of Linguistics: A Study of the Linguistic Theories of B. Malinowski and J.R. Firth.* Cambridge, Mass.: MIT Press, 1968.

Las Casas, B. de. *Historia apologética de las Indias.* English trans. *History of the Indies.* New York: Harper & Row, 1971.

Laubscher, B.J.F. *Sex, Custom, and Psychopathology.* London, 1937.

Leroi-Gourhan, A. *Le geste et la parole.* Paris: Albin Michel, 1964–1965.

Lescarbot, M. *Relations.* Paris, 1610–1612.

Lévi-Strauss, C. "Mythologiques, I," *Le cru et le cuit.* Paris: Plon, 1964.

_____. *Structural Anthropology.* Trans. C. Jacobson. New York: Basic Books, 1963 (1958).

_____. *Les structures élémentaires de la parenté.* Paris: Press Universitaires de France, 1949. English ed. *The Elementary Structures of Kinship.* Boston: Beacon Press, 1969.

———. *Le Totémisme aujourd'hui.* Paris: Presses Univ. de France, 1962.

———. *Tristes Tropiques.* Paris: Plon, 1955.

———. *La Vie familiare et sociale des Indiens Nambikwara,* Paris: Southier, 1948.

Lévy-Bruhl, L. *Les Carnets de L. Lévy-Bruhl (The Notebooks on Primitive Mentality).* Trans. Peter Rivière. New York: Harper & Row, 1975 (1949).

———. *Les fonctions mentales dans les sociétés inférieures.* Paris: Alcan, 1910.

Linton, R. *Culture and Mental Disorders.* G. Devereux, ed. Springfield, Ill.: Thomas, 1956.

———. *The Study of Man.* New York: Appleton-Century, 1936.

———, and Kardiner, A. *The Psychological Frontiers of Society.* Westport, Conn.: Greenwood Press, 1981 (c.1945).

Lowie, R.H. *The Crow Indians.* Farrar & Rinehart, 1935.

———. *The History of Ethnological Theory.* New York: Farrar Rinehart, 1937.

———. *Origin of the State.* New York: Harcourt Brace, 1927.

———. *Primitive Religion.* New York: Liveright, 1948 (c.1924).

———. *Primitive Society.* New York: Boni & Liveright, 1920.

———. *Social Organization.* New York: Rinehart, 1948.

Magli, I. *La femmina dell'uomo.* Bari: Laterza, 1985.

———. *Gesù di Nazaret: Tabù e trasgressione.* Milan: Rizzoli, 1998 (5th ed.).

———. "Il matriarcato come riflesso mitico della cultura," in *Matriarcato e potere delle donne.* Milan: Feltrinelli, 1978. French ed. Paris: Éditions des Femmes, 1979.

———. *Gli uomini della penitenza.* Padua: Muzzio, 1995 (1st ed. 1967).

Maine, H.S.L., *Ancient Law,* London: S. Murray Publications, 1861.

Malinowski, B. *Argonauts of the Western Pacific.* New York: Dutton, 1922.

———. *Coral Gardens and Their Magic.* London: Allan and Unwin, 1935.

———. *Crime and Custom in Savage Society.* London: Routledge and Kegan Paul, 1926.

———. *Culture as Determinant of Behavior.* N.p., 1936.

———. *The Foundations of Faith and Morals.* London: Riddell Memorial Lectures, 1936.

———. "The Group and the Individual in Functional Analysis," *American Journal of Sociology,* XLIV, 1939, pp. 938–964.

———. *The Life of Culture.* N.p., 1927.

———. *Myth as Dramatic Development of Dogma.* N.p., n.d.

———. "The Problem of Meaning in Primitive Languages," in C.K. Ogden and I.A. Richards, *The Meaning of Meaning.* New York: Harcourt, Brace & World, 1963 (1st ed. 1923).

_____. "Science and Religion," in *Magic, Science and Religion and Other Essays*. Westport, Conn.: Greenwood Press, 1984.
_____. *A Scientific Theory of Culture and Other Essays*. Chapel Hill: University of N. Carolina Press, 1944.
_____. *Sex and Repression in Savage Society*. London: Routledge & Kegan Paul, 1927.
_____. *Sex, Culture and Myth*. New York: Harcourt, Brace & World, 1962.
Mandelbaum, D.G., ed. *Language, Culture and Personality*. Berkeley and Los Angeles: University of California Press, 1949.
Manfredi, G. *L'amore e gli amori in J.J. Rousseau*. Milan: Mazzotta, 1978.
Marett, R.R. "Tabu," *Encyclopaedia of Religion and Ethics,* XII. London: Hastings, 1921.
Marino, L. "Wilhelm v. Humboldt e l'antropologia comparata," *Lingua e Stile*, VIII, 1973.
Mauss, M. *The Gift*. New York: Norton, 1967 (1923).
McAlister, L.N. *Spain and Portugal in the New World 1492–1700*. Minneapolis: University of Minnesota Press, 1985.
Mead, M. *Coming of Age in Samoa*. New York: Morrow, 1928.
_____. "The Emergence of the Concept of Personality in the Study of Culture," *Journal of Social Psychology*, V, 1934.
_____. *Male and Female*. New York: Morrow, 1949.
_____. *Sex and Temperament in Three Primitive Societies*. New York: Morrow, 1935.
Meggers, B.J. "Recent Trends in American Ethnology," *American Anthropologist*, XLVIII, pp. 176–214, 1946.
Montesquieu, C.L. de. *L'Esprit des Lois*. Paris: Les Belles Lettres, 1950 (1748).
Moravia, S. *La scienza dell'uomo nel Settecento*. Bari: Laterza, 1970.
_____. *Il tramonto dell'Illuminismo*. Bari: Laterza, 1968.
Morgan, H.L. *Ancient Society*. New York: World Publishing, 1877.
Muller, F.M. *Contributions to the Science of Mythology*. London: Longmans, Green, 1897.
Mumford, L. *Technics and Civilization*. New York: Harcourt, Brace and Company, 1934.
Neumann, E. *The Great Mother: An Analysis of the Archetype*. New York: Macmillan, 1955.
_____. *Zur Psychologie des Weiblichen*. N.p., 1953.
Opler, M.E. *Culture and Mental Health*. New York: Cross Cultural Studies, 1959.
Paulme, D., ed. *Women of Tropical Africa*. London: Routledge and Kegan Paul, 1963.
Pauw, C. de. *Recherches Philosophiques sur les Américains ou Mémoires intéressants pour servir à l'histoire de l'Espèce Humaine*. Berlin, 1768.
Penniman, T.K. *A Hundred Years of Anthropology*. London: Duckworth, 1952.

Petech, L. *I missionari italiani nel Tibet e nel Nepal.* Rome: La Libreria dello Stato, 1952–55, I–VI.
Pettazzoni, R. "Verità del mito," *Studi e Materiali di Storia delle Religioni,* XXI, 1947–48.
Pietro Martire d'Anghiere. *De Orbe Novo.* English trans. New York: Putnam's Sons, 1912.
Poirier, J., ed. *Ethnologie générale.* Paris: Encyclopédie de la Pléiade, Gallimard, 1968.
Polanyi, K. *The Livelihood of Man.* New York: Academic Press, 1977.
Preuss, K.T. *Der religiose Gehalt der Mythen.* Tubingen: J.C.B. Mohr, 1933.
Radcliffe-Brown, A.R. *The Andaman Islanders.* Cambridge: Cambridge University Press, 1922.
_____. *Method in Social Anthropology.* M.N. Srinivas, ed. Chicago: Univrsity of Chicago Press, 1958.
_____. *Structure and Function in Primitive Society.* London: Oxford University Press, 1952; New York: Free Press, 1965.
Radin, P. *The World of Primitive Man.* New York: Schuman, 1953.
Reik, T. *The Psychological Problems of Religion.* New York: Farrar, Straus, 1946 (1919).
Reiler, R.R. ed., *Toward an Anthropology of Women.* New York and London: Monthly Review Press, 1975.
Rivers, W.H. *Kinship and Social Organization.* London: Constable, 1914.
Robertson, W. *The History of America.* London, 1777. Philadelphia: J. Broien and T.L. Plowman, 1812.
Rochemonteix, C. de. *Les Jésuites et la Nouvelle-France au XVII siècle.* Paris: Letouzey et Ané, 1895–96.
Roheim, G. *Psychoanalysis and Anthropology.* New York: International University Press, 1950.
Sahagun, B. de. *A History of Ancient Mexico.* English trans. Detroit: Blaine Etheridge, 1971.
Sapir, E. *Cultural Anthropology and Psychiatry.* N.p., 1932.
_____. *Language: An Introduction to the Study of Speech.* New York: Harcourt, Brace and World, 1921.
_____. *Language and the Woman's Place.* New York: Harper & Row, 1975.
Schmidt, W. *Manuale di storia comparata delle religioni.* Brescia: Morcelliana, 1949.
_____. *Origin and Growth of Religion.* New York: Cooper Square Publishers, 1972 (1922).
Schurtz, H. *Altersklassen und Mannerbunde.* Berlin: Reimer, 1902.
Seymour, M.C. *Mandeville's Travels.* Oxford: Oxford University Press, 1967.
Simpson, G.G. *Life of the Past.* New Haven, Conn.: Yale University Press, 1953.
_____. *This View of Life: The World of an Evolutionist.* New York: Harcourt, Brace and World, 1972.

Sorokin, P.A. *Society, Culture and Personality*. New York: Cooper, 1947.
Spence, S.D. *The Memory Palace of Matteo Ricci*. New York: Viking, 1983.
Spiro, M., ed. *Context and Meaning in Cultural Anthropology*. New York: Free Press, 1965.
Strathern, M. *Women in Between*. London and New York: Seminar Press, 1972.
Street, B.V. *The Savage in Literature*. London: Routledge and Kegan Paul, 1975.
Tacchi Venturi, P., ed. *Opere storiche del padre M. Ricci*. Macerata: Georgetti, 1911–13.
Thwaites, R.G., ed. *The Jesuit Relations and Allied Documents*. New York: Pageant Books, 1959.
Thurnwald, R. *Economics in Primitive Communities*. London: Oxford University Press, 1932.
_____. *L'Esprit humain*. Paris: Payot, 1953.
_____. *Psychologie des Primitiven Menschen*. N.p., 1922.
Todorov, T. *La conquete de l'Amérique: La question de l'autre*. Paris: Éditions du Seuil, 1982.
Topinard, P. *Eléments d'anthropologie générale*. Paris: Delahaye, 1885.
Tylor, E.B. *Anthropology: An Introduction to the Study of Man and Civilization*. New York: Appleton, 1899.
_____. *Primitive Culture*. London: Murray, 1871.
Van der Leeuw, G. *Religion in Essence and Manifestation*. Trans. J.E. Turner. London: Allan and Unwin, 1938 (1933).
Van Gennep, A. *The Rites of Passage*. Trans. S.T. Kimball. Chicago: University of Chicago Press, 1960 (c.1909).
Venturi, F. *L'Antichità svelata e l'idea del Progresso in N.A. Boulanger*. Bari: Laterza, 1947.
Verlinden, C. *The Beginnings of Modern Colonization*. Ithaca, N.Y.: Cornell University Press, 1970.
Volney, C.F. de. *Voyage en Egypte et en Syrie*. Gaulmier, ed. Paris and La Haye: Mouton, 1959.
Waitz, T. *Introduction to Anthropology*. London: Longman, Green, Longman & Roberts, 1863.
Wallerstein, J. *The Modern World System*. New York: Academic Press, 1974.
Webster, H. *Taboo: A Sociological Study*. Stanford: Stanford University Press, 1942.
White, L. "The Ethnology and Ethnography of Franz Boas," *Bulletin of the Texas Memorial Museum*, n. 6, 1963.
_____. *The Science of Culture*. New York: Farrar, Straus and Giroux, 1948.
Wundt, W. *Mythus und Religion*. Leipzig, 1905–1909.
Zahan, D. *La dialectique du verbe chez les Bambara*. Paris and The Hague: Mouton, 1963.

Index

Abbéville, Claude de 28
abortions 124, 158
Abraham, Karl 132
Acapulco 25
accommodation 27
Acosta, José de 43
Adam 9, 32, 33, 44, 129, 157
Africa 15, 33, 39, 45, 69, 121, 149; African man 34, 55
Alexandria 25
Amazonian 60
America 3, 4, 5, 6, 15, 21–23, 24, 25, 30, 33, 34, 39, 41–46, 55, 56, 69, 70, 78, 79, 95, 121, 123, 142, 152, 157, 158; *see also* North America
American Association of Anthropology 110
Amerindian 3, 22, 24, 30, 38, 53, 56, 72, 79, 122, 123
analogy 7, 33, 57, 58, 69, 77, 83, 96, 123, 133, 137, 140, 153, 156, 157
Ancient World 46
Andaman 60, 94, 107
Anglo-Saxon 108
Anthropology Society 62
Aotourou 36, 140
Arabia 24, 50, 53
Arapaho 84
Arbuthnot, Lord John 52
Aretie 77, 149

Argonauts of the Western Pacific 105, 107, 127
Aristotle 2, 10, 11, 34
Asia 9, 10, 26, 34, 39, 45, 51, 69, 74, 121
Asian Society of Calcutta 54
Athenian 31
Attica 75
Augustine of Hippo 13, 130, 138
Austin, John Langshaw 50
Australia 39, 55, 69, 108, 119, 123

Bachofen, Johann Jakob 68, 73–76, 134, 135
Bacon, Roger 13
Balinese 142
Bantu group 96, 155
basic personality 143–146, 152, 158
Basque 53, 55
Bastian, Adolf 68, 69, 75, 76, 133
Bateson, Gregory 142
Baudin, Nicolas 36, 37
Benedict, Ruth 4, 57, 86, 140–143, 145, 146, 149, 151–153
Benzoni, Girolamo 23
Berbers 80
Bergier, Nicolas Sylvestre 40, 113
Berlin 43, 76
Bernard of Chartres 13
Bidney, David 147
Black, Max 50
Bloomfield, Leonard 50

Blumenbach, Johann Friedrich 35, 54
Boas, Franz 3, 4, 50, 56, 57, 58, 73, 77–89, 92, 94, 96, 97, 107–109, 120, 123, 133, 140, 141
Bodin, Jean 29, 45, 75
Bologna 20
Bonn 81
Bopp, Franz 54
Bori cult 154
Bougainville, Louis-Antoine de 14, 36, 37
Boulanger, Antoine Nicolas 14
Brazilians 21
Bréal, Michel 54
Bressani, Francesco Giuseppe 24
British 49, 57, 75, 80, 107
British Association for the Advancement of Science 49
British Columbia 80
Broca, Paul 62, 63
Brosses, Charles de 38, 39, 40, 118
Bruno, Giordano 13
Buffon, Georges-Louis Leclerc 37, 41–46, 64–66
Bunzel, Ruth 87
Burmese 52

Cabot, John 22
Cadiz 23
Caesar, Julius 7, 18
Cairo 25
California 87, 159

171

Index

Canada 15, 24, 30, 32, 33
Canton 25
Cape of Good Hope 39
Cape Verde 23
Capuchins 25
Carletti, Francesco 23, 52
Carothers, J. 150
Cartier, Jacques 21
Cassiodorus 11
Caucasian 55, 62
Celebes 39
Celebi, Evliya 51
Chaldean 24
Charlevoix, Pierre François X. de 33
Chartres 13
Chastellux, François-Jean de 14
Cheyenne Indians 157, 158
China 15, 23, 25–27, 51–53
Chinard, Gilbert 10, 11
Christ (Jesus) 18, 20, 32
Christian 19, 20, 26, 27, 29, 30, 44, 116, 120, 121, 129
Cicero, Marcus Tullius 10, 11
Codrington, Robert Henry 122
Collomb, Henri 150, 155
Columbia University 87
Columbus, Christopher 19, 22
Coman 51
Commerson, Philibert 36, 37
Comte, Auguste 16, 119, 130
Condorcet, Marie-Jean-Antoine Caritat de 13, 66
Confucius 26
Constantinople 51
Cook, James 35–37, 121
Coptic language 24
Coronado, Francisco Vásquez de 22
Council of the Indies 22
Court de Gébelin, Antoine 38
Cracow 97
Crow Indians 92, 94; Foxes 96
Culnacán 22

cuneiform 24
Cuvier, Georges 37, 48, 64–66
Dakar 150, 155
Dalai-Lama 25
Dane 53
Darwin, Charles 62–66, 74
degeneration 29, 32, 33, 42, 44, 45, 54
Degérando, Joseph-Marie 37
Della Valle, Pietro 23
Démeunier, Jean-Nicolas 41
Democritus 10
Descartes, René 2, 13
Devereux, Georges 152, 157–160
Diderot, Denis 14, 36
Dobzhansky, Theodosius 66, 146
Dominicans 20, 21
Dravidians 55
Durkheim, Emile 67, 114–116, 121–123
Dutch 23, 24

East Africa 9
East Indies 23
Eastern World 19, 31
Edelman, Gerard 1
Eden 37
Egypt 8, 9, 25, 46, 53
Ekoi 94
Eldorado 22
Ellis, William 121
Encyclopedists 31, 43, 44
Engels, Friedrich 70–75, 101
England 15, 20, 24, 35, 54, 56, 61, 71
Enlightenment 31, 44, 63, 66
Epicurus 10, 11, 13
Eskimos 10, 11, 13, 60, 77, 85
Ethiopians 10
Ethnological Society of London 49
Ethnological Society of Paris 49
Etienne, Henri 21
Eurasian World 95
Europe 4, 5, 6, 8–10, 15, 17, 19, 20, 21, 22, 23, 25, 26, 28, 34, 35, 36, 40, 41, 43, 44, 45,

51, 52, 54, 56, 61, 80, 114, 116, 121, 123, 126, 129
Eusebius of Caesarea 21
Eve 33, 129, 130

Fantini, B. 66
Far East 29
Fenicio, Giacomo 27
Ferguson, Adam 15, 16
Fernandez (Island) 44
Fijians 36
Firth, Raymond 57
Florence 23, 24
folklore 5, 35, 121, 123
Fonteneau, Alphonse de Saint-Ouge 21
Forster, George 36
Fountain of Youth 22
France 15, 20, 24, 30, 35, 37, 54, 56
Francesco Orazio da Pennabilli 25
Franciscans 20–23, 25, 51
Frazer, James 121
Freud, Sigmund 122, 125, 130–132, 136, 138, 142, 143, 153, 156
Freudian 141, 143, 144, 156, 157

Gadamer, Hans George 147, 148
Gallatin, Albert 56
Garnier, Jean 32
Gatschet, Albert Samuel 56
Gemelli Careri, Francesco 24, 25
Genesis 9
Georgian 52
Germany 15, 20, 23, 25, 53, 56, 60, 62, 71, 73, 75, 77, 83, 114
Giants (biblical) 34, 46
Giovanni da Pian del Carpine 51
Giraud-Teulon, Marc Antoine Louis Felix 74
Goa 23, 25
Goguet, Antoine Yves 14
Golden Age 13, 22
Goldenweiser, Alexander 94
Graebner, Fritz 83

Index

Great Mogul 25
Great Plains 87, 153
Great Wall 25
Greco-Roman 9, 14
Greece 8, 18, 29, 33, 52, 54, 73, 75

Hahn, Eduard 93
Ham 9
Hamito-Semites 55
Harris, Marvin 81
Hausa 154
Hawaiian 93
Hegel, George Wilhelm Friedrich 75
Heidelberg 81
Herder, Johann Gottfried 15, 60
Herodotus 2, 7, 10, 18, 50, 51
Herskovits, Melville J. 109, 110, 146, 147
Hewitt, John N.B. 122
Hidatsa 96
Hippocrates 10
Hitler, Adolf 152
Hoboken 87
Hoebel, Edward Adamson 92
Holland 24
Homer 9
homosexuality 159
Hottentots 55, 96
Hovitt, Alfred William 119
Hubert, René 123
Human Rights Commission 110
Humboldt, Alexander von 38
Humboldt, Wilhelm von 53
Hume, David 118
Hurons 24, 33
Hutton, James 64
Hyperborean Americans 55

Ibn Khaldun 51
ideologues 35, 37, 38, 41
India 15, 23–27, 33, 36, 51, 54, 72, 79, 80, 87, 92, 96, 123, 127, 153, 159
Indies 25, 31
Indo-European 54, 55, 56
Innocent IV, Pope 51

Intorcetta, Prospero 26
Iroquois Indians 24, 33, 60
Irwing, K.F. von 60
Islam 158
Italy 9, 16, 20, 21, 22, 23, 24, 51, 130

Japan 23, 33, 52, 142
Japheth 9
Jauffret, Louis-François 36–38
Javanese 53
Jefferson, Thomas 43
Jesuits 19–21, 24–27, 43
Jesus Christ *see* Christ
Jews 9, 31
Jones, William 54
Judaic-Christian 120, 130
Judaism 31, 32, 119
Jung, Gustav 130, 132, 133
Jurieu, Pierre 31, 32
Jussieu, Joseph de 34

Kaffirs 55
Kant, Immanuel 64
Kardiner, Abram 143, 144
Kathlamet 79
Kiriwina 56, 57
Klemm, Gustave E. 59–62
Kluckhohn, Clyde 60, 61, 88, 152
Kroeber, Alfred Louis 4, 58, 60, 61, 80, 81, 83–85, 87–92, 113, 145
Kula 127, 128
Kwakiutl 79, 85, 152, 153

Lafiteau, Joseph François 14, 30, 32, 33, 46
Lamarck, Jean-Baptiste de Monet 48, 65, 66
Lang, Andrew 119
Laplace, Pierre Simone de 64
Latin 18, 21, 23
Laubscher, B.J.F. 155, 156
Lescarbot, Marc 30
Lettres Persanes 14
Levaillant, François 36
Lévi-Strauss, Claude 58, 94, 103, 116, 125–127, 130, 136, 137, 139
Lévy-Bruhl, Lucien 117, 123, 130
Linnaeus 34
Linton, Ralph 143, 144, 146, 152
Lisbon 23
Livy, Titus 18
logical scheme 88, 89
London 49
Lowie, Robert H. 15, 58, 92–97
Lubbock, John 74, 75, 93, 119
Lucretius 12, 13
Luther, Martin 17
Lyell, Charles 63, 64, 66

Macerata 24
Magli, Ida 20
Mailu 56
Maine, Henry Summer 75
Malabar 27
Malaysians 55, 93
Malinowski, Bronislaw 48–50, 56, 57, 72, 97–107, 109, 125–128, 133, 148
Malta 25
Malthus, Thomas Robert 65
Manila 25
Maori 36, 157, 158
Maragnons 28
Marco da Nizza 22
Marett, Robert Ranulph 122
Marseilles 37
Marx, Karl 70, 71, 74, 101
Marxist 5, 101
Matriarchy 68, 74, 75, 96, 134, 135
Maupertuis, Pierre-Louis Moreau de 65
Mauss, Marcel 103, 121, 123
McGill University 150
McLennan, John F. 68, 76
Mead, Margaret 4, 80, 86, 141, 142, 145, 146
Mediterranean 9, 55
Meiners, Christopher 15, 60

Melanesians 103, 104, 122, 127
menstruation 96, 124, 126
Mercure de France 36
Mesopotamia 24
Mexico 22, 46, 87, 123
Michaelis, Johann David 53
Minden 77
minimum effort (principle of) 17, 18
Mocquet, Jean 28
model *see* pattern
Mohave Indians 159
Molina, Father Luis de 43
Moluccan 39
monastic orders 19, 52
Mongolian 51, 55
Montaigne, Michel Eyquem de 42
Montesquieu, Charles 14, 29–31, 43, 75
monthly cycle *see* menstruation
Montreal 150
Morgan, Lewis Henry 15, 16, 69–74, 76, 88, 89, 92, 93
Moses 29, 73
Muller, Friedrich 55
Muller, Max 55
music 137

Nambikwara 126, 127
Naples 25
Nepal 25
Neumann, Erich 133, 134, 135
New France 24, 30, 33
New Guinea 127, 141
New Jersey 87
New World 21, 41
Newton, Isaac 64
Niebuhr, Carsten. 53
Nile 9
Nobili, Roberto de 26, 27
Northern people 9
North America 21, 29, 72, 87, 95; *see also* America
North Asian 95
Nouvelle Cythère (Tahiti) 36
Nubians 55

Observateurs de l'Homme 35–37, 41, 49
obvious (principle of the) 11, 17, 93, 116, 127, 147
Oceania 37
Odyssey 10
Oedipus 107, 125, 132, 143
Old Testament 29, 32, 114
Old World 41
Opler, Morris 156
orders, religious 19–21, 25, 29, 51, 52; *see also* monastic orders
Orient 9, 24, 27, 33

Pacific 36, 97, 105, 121, 127
Pacific Northwest 85
Padua 20
Pan-African Conference of Psychiatry 155
papacy 19
Papuan 36, 55, 127
Paris 21, 30, 36, 37, 49, 62, 87, 140
Parkinson, Sydney 36
Pascal, Blaise 13
Patagonian 46
pattern 12, 18, 56, 111, 112, 120, 133, 140, 143, 145, 148, 150–152, 155, 157, 158
Paul (Saint) 18
Pauw, Cornelius de 15, 43–46
Persepolis 25
Persia 24, 25, 51
personality-culture 86, 88, 138, 141, 156
Peru 46, 69, 87
Pettazzoni, Raffaele 118, 130, 131
Philippines 25
Pietro Martire d'Anghiera 22
Pigafetta, Antonio Vincenzo 51
Plato 10
Poland 56, 97
Polynesia 38, 80, 94, 121, 122
Polo, Marco 51
Pontifical State 19
Pope 19, 20
Portugal 20, 23

Post, Albert 76
potency (plane of) 5, 112, 113, 115–118, 120–123, 127, 128, 136–138
Potlatch 80, 93
Poutrincourt, Baron J. de 30
Preuss, Konrad Theodor 120, 122
Prichard, James Cowles 65
Priscian of Caesarea 11
progress 8, 10, 11–15, 42, 44, 46, 55, 59–61, 63, 67, 81, 83, 116, 147, 149, 161
projections 1, 112, 113, 115, 118, 131, 138
Propaganda Fide Congregation 25
Psychopathologie Africaine 150
pygmies 9, 10, 34

Quebec 24
Quine, Willard 50

race 10, 28, 29, 34, 35, 54–56, 59, 61–63, 65, 67, 75, 78–81, 98, 99, 139
racism 62, 135
Radcliffe-Brown, Alfred Reginald 107–109
Ramusio, Giambattista 22
Rank, Otto 132
Ratzel, Friedrich 69, 75, 76
Raynal, Guillaume Thomas François 40
reciprocity (of the Trobriands) 103
Reformation 20
Relativism 15, 107, 109, 146, 148, 159, 160
Renan, Ernest 54, 55
rhetoric (of language) 18
Revelation 29, 30, 32, 33, 65, 119
Ricci, Matteo 26, 52
Rivers, William Halse 89
Robertson, William 45, 46
Roheim, Geza 156, 157
Romans 11, 14, 29
Romanticism 54, 71, 116
Rome 19, 20, 23–26, 73
Rouen 21

Rousseau, Jean-Jacques 14, 42, 45, 54, 116, 139
Russia 51

Sagard, Gabriel 28
Saint Helena (Island) 23
St. Mark (Public Library of Venice's Republic)
Samoa 141
Sanskrit 23, 49, 51, 54
Sapir, Edward 4, 57, 58, 150
Sassetti, Filippo 23, 51
savage 15, 33, 36, 46, 55, 66, 103, 104, 125, 126; good 22, 30, 36, 44
Schiaparelli, Ernesto 9
schizophrenia 149
Schlegel, Friedrich von 54
Schmidt, Wilhelm 32, 94, 97, 119
Schurtz, Heinrich 76, 95, 96
Scythians 51
Secret Societies 32, 95, 96
Semitic 32, 55
Seneca 10, 11
Seville 23
Shem 9
Siberian 95, 159
Simpson, George Gaylord 65
situational context 57
Smith, William 65
Société Linguistique of Paris 54
Society of African Psychopathology 150
Sonora 23
South America 29, 80, 92, 137
Spain 20, 22, 25, 45
Spencer, Herbert 64, 66, 119

Spencer, John 31, 32
Statement on Human Rights 110
Strabo 71
Strait of Magellan 39
Stuttgart 68
Sudan 9
Swedish 34
Swin 56
Syria 53

Tacchi-Venturi, Pietro 26
Tacitus 7, 18
Tahiti 36, 37, 140
Taine, Hippolyte 75
Tamil 52
Tartars 15, 51
tattoos 21
Ten Commandments 29
Teotihuacan 25
Thevet, André 21, 28
Thoms, William John 35
Thurnwald, Richard 76
Tibet 25
Transcultural Psychiatric Research 150
Trobriands 56, 97, 103, 125
Tunisian 51
Tupinambas 21
Turgot, Anne Robert Jacques 13
Turkey 24, 25, 75
Tylor, Edward Burnett 2, 8, 40, 56, 60, 61, 67, 72–74, 76, 95, 111–119

United Nations 110
United States 53

Vancouver 36
Van Gennep, Arnold 95
Venice 22
Vera Cruz 25

Vespucci, Amerigo 22
Vicenza 51
Vico, Giambattista 16, 52, 130, 131
Vienna 25
Vierkandt, Alfred 76, 120
Virchow, Rudolf 81
Volney, Constantin-François de 38, 53
Voltaire (François-Marie Arouet) 15, 31, 40, 45, 60
Vossius, Gerardus Johannis 29

Waitz, Theodor 59, 62
Wallis, Samuel 37
Warburton, William 38
Webster, Hutton 95
Wells, William 65
Western 6, 9, 14, 19, 22, 26, 28, 30, 32, 33, 44, 50, 56, 65, 105, 123, 124, 127, 134, 135, 137, 147, 148, 149, 151, 155, 156
White, Leslie 78
Whorf, Benjamin L. 58
Williams, W. 122
Wittenberg theses 17
Wittgenstein, Ludwig 50
Wittkower, Erich D. 150
Wolof 155
World Congress of Psychiatry 149
World Congress of Social Psychiatry 150
World Health Organisation 150
Wundt, Wilhelm 113, 115, 117, 120, 130, 131

Yale 97

Zeitschrift fur volker psychologie 62